THE SURVIVAL GUIDE FOR

MaKiNg aNd BeiNg FrieNds

James J. Crist, Ph.D.

free spirit
PUBLISHING®

Library of Congress Cataloging-in-Publication Data
Crist, James J.
   The survival guide for making and being friends / by James J. Crist, PhD.
         pages cm
         Summary: "Helps kids improve their social skills and friendship skills. Advice covers topics such as breaking the ice, developing friendships, overcoming problems, and more"— Provided by publisher.
   Includes bibliographical references and index.
   ISBN 978-1-57542-472-9 (paperback) — ISBN 1-57542-472-X (paperback) 1. Friendship in children—Juvenile literature. 2. Friendship—Juvenile literature. 3. Interpersonal relations in children—Juvenile literature. 4. Interpersonal relations—Juvenile literature. I. Title.
   BF575.F66C75 2014
   177'.62—dc23
                                                                                    2014020503

Edited by Eric Braun
Cover and interior design by Tasha Kenyon and Michelle Lee Lagerroos
Illustrations by Jimmy Holder

Printed in China

Free Spirit Publishing
An imprint of Teacher Created Materials
9850 51st Avenue, Suite 100
Minneapolis, MN 55442
(612) 338-2068
help4kids@freespirit.com
freespirit.com

FSC
www.fsc.org
MIX
Paper | Supporting
responsible forestry
FSC® C144853

Free Spirit offers competitive pricing.
Contact edsales@freespirit.com for pricing information on multiple quantity purchases.

Dedication

I dedicate this book to all the kids and teens I have worked with over the past 20 years who have struggled with making and keeping friends. You were my inspiration for everything in its pages. Having friends is one of the greatest joys in life, and I hope that I am able to help even more kids by writing this book.

Acknowledgments

I'd like to thank my incredibly supportive parents, who understood how important it was to me to maintain my friendships, even when it meant borrowing the car again and again to do so! I'd like to thank Carter Ferrington, who gave me the idea for writing this book. I would like to thank my niece, Kiera Crist, for her initial review of the manuscript and giving me some excellent suggestions. Finally, I would like to thank my editor, Eric Braun, for always making my writing more kid-friendly, and all the staff at Free Spirit who continue to believe in me and support my writing.

CONTENTS

A Friendly Introduction 1

Chapter 1 What's the Big Deal
About Friends? 6
What Is a Friend? 7
What Else Is Good About Friends? 8
What Does It Take to Make and Be Friends? 11

Chapter 2 Ten Steps for Meeting
and Making New Friends 14
1. Put Yourself in the Right Place 15
2. Check for Shared Interests 16
3. Greet People 18
4. Start Conversations 20
5. Ask About the Other Person 21
6. Talk About Yourself 24
7. Notice How Others React 25
8. Keep the Conversation Going 27
9. Join Group Conversations 29
10. Say Good-Bye 30

Chapter 3 Seven Tips for Growing
Friendships (And Four Friendship
Flubs to Avoid) 33
Tip #1: Share 34
Tip #2: Help 34
Tip #3: Take Turns 35

Tip #4: Give Compliments.. 35

Tip #5: Ask for Advice or Help... 36

Tip #6: Develop a New Interest.. 38

Tip #7: Stick Up for Others... 39

Four Friendship Flubs to Avoid.. 41

Practice Makes Perfect.. 44

Chapter 4 Strengthen Your Social Skills— and Your Friendships

Chapter 4 Strengthen Your Social Skills— and Your Friendships 46

Friendship Levels.. 47

Start Slow, Then Get Closer 49

Friends of the Opposite Sex, Different Backgrounds, or Different Ages 50

Using Social Etiquette.. 51

Showing Empathy... 52

Staying in Touch 54

Being a Good Sport 55

Networking 57

Avoid These Politeness Pitfalls 59

Chapter 5 Put Together
Great Get-Togethers 63

Inviting Others 64

When You Are Invited 70

Keep Things Going 73

Chapter 6 How Autism, ADHD,
and Other Conditions Can Affect
Friendships 75

What's a Disorder? 76

Being the Friend of Someone with a Disorder 79

If You're the One with the Disorder 81

Chapter 7 How to Handle Fights,
Hurt Feelings, and Other Friendship
Troubles 85

What Happened, Anyway? 86

Talking It Out 88

When Your Friend Is the One Who's Upset 90

Forgiveness 92

Fixing the Problem 93

Chapter 8 When Friendships End 96

Why Friendships End 97

Signs That It Might Be Time to End a Friendship 99

It's Time to Talk 100

Could You Be the Hurtful One? 102

Ending a Friendship 103

When Someone Else Ends the Friendship 106

Chapter 9 The Next Step:
Being the Best Friend You Can Be...............108

Including Others.. 109

Organizing... 110

Mixing and Matching 112

Volunteering.. 112

Standing Up... 113

Index 116

About the Author 119

A FRieNdLy INTROdUCTiON

What are a few of your favorite things to do? Do you love to ride your bike? Surf the Internet? Do puzzles? Play games with character dolls or action figures? Do you get excited about hiking, swimming, or singing? Maybe you like to watch funny movies, chomp on popcorn, and laugh until you cry.

Whatever you love to do, chances are it's a lot more fun to do with a friend.

Think about it. Board games, video games, school, sports, music, handstands, summer camp, cooking, hide and seek, burp jokes, long car rides, short subway rides, TV shows, YouTube videos, chores, and eating pizza. All these activities are probably going to be more satisfying if you share them with a friend.

And it's not just about fun. Friends can support you when you feel down. They can remind you what you're good at and help you get better at other things. Friends help each other, stick up for each other, and listen to each other. Friends play together, talk together, and just hang out and do nothing together. Sure, sometimes friends fight—but then they make up, and their friendship has a chance to be stronger than ever.

Some kids find it natural to socialize and build relationships. Other kids are shy at first, but do okay once they get to know someone. And some kids are uncomfortable in social situations, or they just haven't learned the best ways to start friendships and keep them going. They struggle to make friends.

How about you? Does making, keeping, and being friends come easily to you? Answer the following questions to get an idea.

A Friendly Quiz

For each question, give yourself 1 point for "definitely," 2 for "sometimes," or 3 for "hardly ever." Write your answers on a sheet of paper.

1 = Definitely   2 = Sometimes   3 = Hardly Ever

1   It's easy for me to walk up to someone I don't know and start talking.

2   I think I'm pretty good at making friends.

3   I usually keep friends for a long time.

4   I'm good at apologizing when I accidentally hurt a friend's feelings.

5   I know how to handle problems with friends when they happen.

6   Lots of people seem to want to be my friend.

7   I have a "best friend" and we get along great.

8   I get invited to friends' homes and invite them to mine.

9   I am a good sport when I play games with my friends.

10   I can stick up for a friend if he or she is in trouble.

Add up your scores. If you got between 10 and 15 points, congratulations! You're a confident friend-maker with strong friendship skills. Keep reading to learn how to improve your skills even more—and how to take them to the next level.

If you got 16 or more points, don't worry. You can use some improvement in your friendship skills, but so can most people. And notice that I am calling them friendship *skills*. That's because making friends, developing strong friendships, and being a good friend are just like snowboarding, swimming, biking, writing, playing video games, dancing, and being a good student. They are all skills that you can practice and get better at. It's true that some people have a natural talent for socializing. Some people seem to attract friends the way your Halloween candy attracts grabby parents. (Why don't they just buy their own?)

But even people who have an easy time with friendship have to practice. And *everyone* can improve.

As a psychologist, I work with lots of kids and help them figure out ways of living happier and healthier lives. For many of them, that means improving their social skills. That's why I wrote this book. I want to help *you* be happier and healthier. I know how important friendship is, and I know how hard it can be sometimes. The skills you'll learn in this book are some of the same ones I teach the kids I see in my work.

There's another reason I wrote this book. I was a shy kid. I missed some great chances to make friends because I didn't have the nerve—or the skills—to join other kids in their fun. What if they didn't like me? Or laughed at me? What if we didn't get along? I also didn't know how to work out problems with friends. But as I grew older, I learned. And I realized I didn't want to miss out anymore, so I developed my friendship skills and practiced. Now I have lots of friends, even though I can still be shy when meeting new people.

Maybe you wish you had more friends, and you need help getting to know people. Or maybe you're happy with the number of friends you have, but you need advice for getting along and solving arguments. Or maybe you're not sure: You feel pretty good about your friendships, but sometimes you feel left out, lonely, or confused.

This book can help you with all of those situations and more. You can learn how to meet kids, make friends, become better friends, settle arguments, and understand each other. You can learn how to act when you get together, the importance of being a good sport, and how you can make your friendships last for years—if that's what you want. And you'll learn how to end friendships when they don't work out and it becomes time to say good-bye. (It's sad, but once in a while "breaking up" is the best thing for everyone.)

The last chapter is all about being a "super" friend—someone who makes friends from different social groups, brings different friends together, stands up against bullying, and helps other kids feel good about themselves. That kind of friend is a leader, and anybody can be one.

Feel free to dip into any chapter where you might need some extra help right now. For example, if you're having an argument with a friend that you just can't seem to solve, skip ahead to Chapter 7, "How to Handle Fights, Hurt Feelings, and Other Friendship Troubles." For the best understanding of all things friendship, start with Chapter 1 and read all the way through.

Every chapter opens with a "What would you do?" story about kids having some kind of struggle with friendship. But these stories don't have endings. Instead, they end with a question for you: What would *you* do? After you read the chapter, you'll have the chance to revisit the story and make your own ending.

To help you learn all the skills and tips in every chapter, you'll also find a few other features:

* **Friendship Phrases.** Plenty of helpful examples of how to use the skills you're learning will be marked with this talk balloon:

* **Try This!** Sort of like homework assignments, these are little things you can do to practice what you learn.

★**He and She**

All of the information in this book is meant for both boys and girls. When giving examples or explaining an idea, I change the pronoun I use from section to section—starting with "she," then "he," then "she" again, and so on. No matter which pronoun I use in a particular example, remember that it is meant for you.

* **Quotes from Real Kids.** These are words of advice and friendship stories from kids I've worked with.

* **Quick Quizzes.** At the end of every chapter, take a short quiz to see what you learned.

I'd like to know how my book helps you. I'd love to hear about your challenges and successes with friends. You can email me at help4kids@freespirit.com or send me a letter at:

Dr. James Crist
c/o Free Spirit Publishing
6325 Sandburg Road, Suite 100
Minneapolis, MN 55427-3674

Chapter 1

What's The Big Deal About Friends?

Devon, age 10, goes outside for recess at school. He brings his game cards and plays with them alone. He thinks the kids at his school are all bullies. He thinks, "I'm fine. I don't need friends." He figures it won't work out anyway, so why even try? But after a while, he looks over and sees the other kids playing tag and laughing and joking. He tries to tell himself he doesn't care, but inside, he does. It's hard to play alone all the time.

What would you do?

Devon seems pretty unhappy. What would you do if you were in his shoes? You'll find some ideas in this chapter, and at the end of the chapter you'll have a chance to revisit Devon's story and make up an ending for it.

Human beings are "social creatures." That means we have a built-in need to be social—to get to know each other and build relationships. Since the first humans walked the earth, we have lived in communities. We take care of each other. We keep each other company. We love each other.

From the moment we're born, it's in our nature to be happier when we're together, at least some of the time. We get some of that companionship from our families. But we also make important connections with others—our friends.

What Is a Friend?

We all have different things we look for in a friend. Here are a few things that many people value. You can probably think of other ideas to add to the list.

A friend is someone you can do things with:

* play
* hang out
* explore
* tell stories
* share important news
* laugh
* cry
* learn new things together

A friend is also someone you can:

* learn new things *from*
* count on when you have a problem
* support when she has a problem

Friends are not only fun, helpful, and reliable. They're also good for you! People who have friends are more likely to:

* be happier
* be healthier
* do better in school
* live longer
* be more successful at their jobs when they grow up

Yup—live longer! Hard to believe? Maybe so, but it's true.

What Else Is Good About Friends?

Lots of things.

Friendships help you learn to deal with your feelings. When you have friends, it's normal to disagree, argue, have your feelings hurt, and apologize when you've messed up. Friends also have to learn to share, take turns, work together, and compromise. As you learn how to do these things successfully, you're growing up. You're learning how to get along in the world. Learning to get along now will help you be happier in the future.

When you make friends and manage relationships, you compare yourself to others. You see what others think of you, and you learn a lot about yourself that way. Maybe you don't think you're very smart, but a friend thinks it's cool how you can take things apart and fix them. You may start to see yourself as smart. Or maybe you joke around a lot when you're supposed to be listening or working. Your friends like your sense of humor, but they ask you to be quiet when it's time to focus. You're learning how to act in different situations.

Friends Around the World

How do you say "friend" in other languages? Just say the word to someone who speaks a different language, and they'll know you're interested in talking to them.

	Say it like
Spanish: *amigo* (boy) or *amiga* (girl)	uh-ME-go, uh-ME-guh
French: *ami*	ah-ME
German: *freund*	FROYND
Italian: *amico* (boy) or *amica* (girl)	ah-ME-co, ah-ME-cuh
Arabic: *sadiqi* (boy) or *sadiqati* (girl)	sah-dee-KEY, sah-dee-KA-tee
Russian: *drug* (boy), *podruga* (girl)	DROOG, pah-DROO-guh
Chinese: *péngyou*	pung-YO
Japanese: *tomodachi*	tow-moh-da-chee
Indian (Hindi): *dost*	DOST

Learning how to get along with people can help you in other ways. For example, you may do well in your schoolwork, but if you can't get along with your teachers, it will make going to school a lot harder for you. If you lose your cool and yell, forgetting that you are hurting people's feelings, you might even get into serious trouble.

When you grow up, friends are still important. You'll want to have friends who can help you when you need it, give you rides to places, go with you to the movies, celebrate your birthday, shoot baskets with you, or even just talk. And speaking of when you grow up, getting along with others is also important when you have a job.

What Does It Take to Make and Be Friends?

You already know that people are social creatures. It makes sense, then, that making and being friends require "social skills." These are the different abilities and techniques we all use to get along.

Just like playing an instrument, throwing a ball, or being a good student, social skills are learnable. And just like those other skills, you can't expect to have super social skills overnight. You have to practice. The more you practice, the better you'll get.

Friendship also requires the ability to look closely at yourself. If you have trouble with friendships, ask yourself why. This can be hard. It takes courage, but it's worth it, and you can do it. Be honest with yourself. Maybe you are shy or don't have strong social skills yet. Or maybe you sometimes act in ways that make it harder for others to like you. Some kids might be rude, bossy, or mean. They might not show good sportsmanship, or they might have trouble sharing or taking turns. Some kids are too rough with other kids. Is that ever you?

If you aren't sure what the problem is, ask someone you trust. This might be a parent, teacher, counselor, or friend. Be open to what the person tells you. It might hurt your feelings to hear it, but it's an important first step. How else are you going to get better at making friends? You have to know what to work on.

> "It can be good to have a circle of friends, but if it gets too big, you can feel excluded. I think a group of four or five friends is best." —Girl, age 12

You may also want to think about what kind of friendships you want. Some kids like to have a lot of friends. They are very social and hang out with all kinds of different people. Other kids prefer to have only a few close friends. Some kids have a best friend, others don't. Some kids hate to be alone, so they spend all their free time with other kids. Some people need "alone time" to recharge, and they hang out with friends less often. All these preferences are fine. Think about what *yours* is.

? What would you do?

Remember Devon (page 6), who is afraid to join in with the other kids at school? He tells himself that he doesn't need friends. He tells himself that he's fine without them.

In this chapter, you learned a lot of reasons why friends are important. You learned that friends can help us in many ways, and friendship is an important way of growing up. And you learned that not everyone is naturally good at making friends—but everyone can get better.

So what would you do if you were Devon?

You probably guessed that Devon would be happier if he found the courage to talk to some other kids. Make up some things he could say that would help him do that.

Quick Quiz

Take this short quiz to see how much you learned by reading this chapter. If you like, write your answers on a sheet of paper.

TRUE or FALSE?

1 You can learn more about yourself by making friends.

2 People who have friends tend to live longer.

3 Even kids who have trouble making friends can get better at it.

4 Asking others if you act in ways that make it harder to form friendships can be helpful.

5 True "social skills" can only be gained by playing the online video game "Social Skillz Crush."

Let's see how you did.

The answer to the first four questions is **True**. The answer to question 5 is "Of course not!"

Chapter 2

Ten Steps For Meeting and Making New Friends

Sasha, age 12, sits by herself at lunch every day. She wants to eat with the other girls in her class, but all the seats are taken and no one asks her to join them. After a while, she finally gets up the nerve to walk toward one of the tables. But everyone there is talking and laughing, and even though there is one seat open, she's afraid to interrupt them and ask if it's okay to sit there. She just stands there and the other kids begin to stare. Sasha feels foolish and isn't sure what to do.

? What would you do?

Do you think Sasha should wait until the kids invite her to sit? Should she ask the kids if she can join them? Should she just sit down? Or should she give up and walk away? We'll come back to Sasha later in this chapter—see if you get some new ideas as you read on.

Making friends is a lot like any other goal you have in life. It helps to break it down into smaller parts or steps. This chapter shows you how to get to know new friends with confidence.

① Put Yourself in the Right Place

The first step to making new friends is figuring out where you can find them. Look around you! You can make new friends in your classroom; at your church, mosque, or synagogue; in your neighborhood; on your sports team; in your scout group; on the playground—anywhere you are where other kids are around. Friends of your parents might also have kids your age. You can ask your parents to plan a get-together for your families. These are all great ways to meet people who might have similar interests as you.

★ Try This!

Check out the kids who are really good at making friends. Some people seem to have a natural talent for friendship—they can't help being social. Maybe they're funny, talkative, great at sports, or just plain nice. You might get a few good ideas for socializing by watching these kids.

Pay attention to:
- how they greet others
- what they talk about
- how they handle problems
- how they respond to what other kids say
- how often they talk to others
- how often they smile

As you watch them, think about what you can learn from their actions. You don't want to copy them, but you might get ideas for doing things that work for you.

The beginning of the school year or the first couple meetings of a club, team, or other group are great times to make new friends. That's because not everyone knows each other, so they are more open to meeting new people.

② Check for Shared Interests

The next step is to look for kids you have something in common with. After all, if you don't like many of the same things, you won't have much to talk about or do together. Chances are you won't become friends, or at least not close friends.

The place where you meet the other kids might give you a clue about what you have in common. If you're in chess club, for example, chances are you all like chess. Take a chance and talk with your teammates about the game. You can use time between matches or even during matches to talk to the other club members. Cheering them on when they do well or telling them "nice try" when they don't can also be good ways to break the ice with other kids.

Other interests you might share include your taste in music, TV shows, video games, fun websites, books, sports, and musical instruments. Listen to what kids talk about and what they do. These are good ways of learning about someone.

Sometimes, friendships start when you just join the fun. You can find out later what you have in common. If you'd like to join kids who are playing something, wait for a break in the game, like when they are switching sides. Then simply ask to join. You can say something like:

* "Can I join?"
* "Do you need another player?"
* "Mind if I play too?"

★ Try This!

It's normal to feel anxious when you go up to a new person or group. You might notice that your stomach hurts, or that your hands are shaking. These are signs of anxiety or nervousness. Two ways to calm yourself when you're nervous are doing deep breathing and using positive self-talk.

Deep Breathing
Practice this at home: Take five deep breaths in through your nose and out through your mouth. This will help calm you so you feel less nervous. Once you get the hang of it, you can do it before you go up to kids in a social situation.

Positive Self-Talk
Instead of telling yourself that you can't do it, give yourself a pep talk. Research shows that when we say positive things to ourselves, we feel more confident and have higher self-esteem. Just tell yourself something like:

- I can do this!
- I will give it my best shot.
- The worst thing that could happen is that they say no. I will be fine.
- I am a good friend.

If they say agree, say "Thanks!" Introduce yourself so everyone will know who you are. If you're playing a game, focus on the game. This isn't the time to get to know the players better. That will come later. Be sure to thank them for letting you play when you're finished. And of course, be a good sport. (Check out Chapter 4 for more information on being a good sport.)

There's a chance the kids will say no when you ask to join them. Maybe they don't have room in the game for another player. Or maybe they don't want to add a new player to a game that has started already. If that happens, don't get discouraged, and try not to act mad. That won't help. Just say, "Okay—if you need someone later, let me know. Have fun!"

Being able to take a "no" without getting upset tells the other kids that you can handle rejection. You show them that you're mature and probably play fair without blowing up or pouting. And maybe they'll want you to play next time!

③ Greet People

Once you've figured out who you'd like to get to know, it's time to greet them. This is often the hardest part for shy kids. It helps to have a plan for how to begin a conversation. And it helps to practice.

As for your plan, there's no need to get too fancy. Start out by just saying "Hi!" Saying hi to people you see while looking at them and smiling (don't leave out the smiling part) shows that you're friendly. It also makes others happy.

Sometimes you don't even have to say anything: A simple nod can be enough to show you've seen someone. Other ways to say hello include waving and giving a high five or fist bump. This lets others know that you're happy to see them. Whatever way you decide to greet someone, be sure to make eye contact. That's an

★ Try This!

Make a point of saying hi to several people every day. Say it to people in the hall, to your teacher when you walk into class, to the bus driver when you get on the bus, to the cashier at the store checkout, to your parents when they walk in the door, or to your neighbors when you walk down the street. You can say hi to dogs whose owners are walking them! "Hi" works even better when you follow it with "How are you?" or "How's it going?" or "What's up?"

important sign that you're friendly and interested in the other person.

Before approaching someone, pay attention to what she's doing and who she's talking to. Notice if she seems friendly or not so friendly. Friendly kids smile a lot. Kids who are not so friendly argue and make fun of each other.

Next, walk closer to the person or group. If the group is talking, stand close by and wait for an opening. Don't interrupt people when they're in the middle of talking. Wait for a break in conversation, when no one is talking for at least a few seconds. If someone looks or smiles at you, that's a good sign that the person is open to talking.

If you see someone alone, that's a great time to approach her and say something.

Introducing yourself is pretty simple. Make sure you give your name and ask for hers. Keep it simple: "Hi, my name is Alex. What's your name?" When you get the other person's name, repeat it back: "Hi, Jenny—nice to meet you!"

> "I heard two girls talking about the weather and how they hoped there would be no school tomorrow. I said I wanted it to snow and we made up a game about it and we became friends." —Girl, age 9

"If I saw a kid sitting alone, especially if he was a new student, I'd sit next to him and ask if he wanted to be my friend. I'd keep him company." —Boy, age 9

4 Start Conversations

Now it's time to talk. If you see people already talking, try to say something related to what they are talking about. Sometimes joining a conversation that's already started can be an easy way to start talking with people.

If you're starting a new conversation, pick a good time and place. You can't have much of a conversation in the hallway right before the bell rings or in between classes—there isn't enough time. At lunch or recess, or before or after school, are good times to talk.

Here are a few ideas for starting a conversation. You can talk about:

* the weather

* something fun you did recently

* special events at school, such as parties or dances

* sporting events, such as the football game you saw on Sunday

* places you've visited

* pets (dogs, cats, fish, tarantulas)

* things you plan on doing or places you plan on going to soon

* favorite games, foods, places, TV shows, sports

★ **Try This!**
The next time you go to class, practice, or a club meeting, introduce yourself to someone you don't know. Before or after class (or the practice or meeting) are both good times. You may also have some free time during class when you're allowed to talk. If you introduce yourself in class, that makes it much easier to start a conversation at a later time.

How does this work? You can say something or ask a question. Here are some ways you can try. The more you practice starting conversations, the easier it will get.

* ✳ "I'm sure glad it's not raining again."
* ✳ "What did you think of that math test? I thought it was tough!"
* ✳ "Did you see the hockey game on Sunday?"
* ✳ "How's it going?"
* ✳ "What's new?"
* ✳ "What have you been up to?"
* ✳ "Have you done anything fun lately?"
* ✳ "What's up?"
* ✳ "What did you do over the weekend?"
* ✳ "Nice puppy—what's its name?"

One more tip about conversations: Watch your personal space. Most people stay about an arm's length away from one another when they're talking. Getting too close to someone invades people's personal space and makes them feel uncomfortable.

5 Ask About the Other Person

After you start talking to someone, the next step is to learn more about each other. In a way, getting to know someone by asking questions is like being a reporter or an interviewer. You want to show that you are interested in the person, but you also want to make sure the person is comfortable talking to you.

Here are some good questions to ask people when you are getting to know them:

✳ "What do you like to do for fun?"

✳ "What are your favorite TV shows or videos?"

✳ "What video games do you like?"

✳ "Do you play any sports?"

✳ "Where do you live?"

✳ "What's your favorite food?"

✳ "Are you in band? What do you play?"

✳ "Do you like school? What's your favorite subject?"

If the person shares something that you have in common, that makes it easier to keep the conversation going. Say, "Me, too!" and share something about the same subject. If you don't learn what you have in common right away, keep asking questions. But don't overdo it. Be sure to mix in comments with your questions. Here's an example:

✳ **Daijon:** Do you play sports?

✳ **Aaron:** Yeah, I play soccer.

✳ **Daijon:** Cool. Soccer is fun but I like baseball better.

✳ **Aaron:** Baseball is great. What team do you play for?

✳ **Daijon:** My school team. What soccer team do you play on?

✳ **Aaron:** The Thunder. How long have you been playing baseball?

✳ **Daijon:** Four years now.

✳ **Aaron:** Wow—that's a long time. What position do you play?

✳ **Daijon:** Shortstop and pitcher. How about you?

✳ **Aaron:** Mostly goalie and some wing.

Notice how the conversation goes back and forth. That keeps it moving. Notice also the nice things the boys say to each other ("Wow!" and "Cool!"). Saying something encouraging keeps the other person interested in talking.

Another way to think of it is to ask questions that start with who, what, when, where, why, or how. That will give you a lot of information about the person you're trying to become friends with. Here are some examples:

★**Try This!**

Next time you're talking with a new friend, or even an old one, choose one of the topics below and ask what her favorite is. After she answers, ask her why. This can be a fun way to get someone talking—and get to know that person better.

What's your favorite . . .

- animal?
- fruit?
- sport?
- TV show?
- video game?
- book?
- singer or band?
- character from a movie, show, or book?
- place to visit?
- school subject?
- hobby?

✳ "**Who** do you usually hang out with?"

✳ "**What** are you doing this weekend?"

✳ "**Where** did you go last weekend?"

✳ "**When** did you first start Girl Scouts?"

✳ "**Why** did you decide to learn taekwondo?"

✳ "**How** did you get to be so good at piano?"

6 Talk About Yourself

When you feel comfortable asking questions and commenting on other people's answers, then you are ready to share some things about yourself. Try to keep your comments on topic. For example, if kids at lunch are talking about playing dodgeball at recess and you interrupt to tell them about a video game you like, they're going to feel confused. Instead, add to the conversation about dodgeball or wait for a pause in the conversation before starting a new topic.

By listening to what other kids are talking about, you will get a better idea of common interests you share with them. Try to talk about things you and the other kids like first. This will create a connection between you and them. Later, you can share more about things you like and see if the others are interested. If you're not sure, ask. "Want to hear more about my gymnastics routine?" This gives the other people a chance to say no. Don't take it too personally—just move on to something else.

And it's okay if you like different things. One of the fun things about having friends with different interests is that you can learn about new things you would not have known about otherwise.

Sharing things about yourself is a great way to let others get to know you and learn to like you. But try not to talk too much about yourself or "hog" the conversation. After you share a little bit about yourself, go back to asking about the other person.

⑦ Notice How Others React

One of the most important things to remember when you're having a conversation

★**Being Turned Down**

Sometimes people will tell you no. They won't want to hear about your computer game, or they won't want to make bracelets with you. They won't accept an invitation to your house, or they won't let you join their game of kickball. You might be disappointed or maybe even mad. Your feelings might be hurt. But the good news is, much of the time, kids will say yes. You just have to try again. If a kid turns you down for something, remember that you'll have another chance—at a later time or with another person. Take a deep breath and say, "Okay, maybe next time. See you later!" Stay positive, and keep on asking people.

is to be sure the other person is interested in what you're saying. Signs that someone is interested include:

* making eye contact with you—looking you in the eye

* smiling at you

* asking you questions about what you're talking about

* showing excitement or enthusiasm

* sharing something similar to what you are saying

If the other person is doing some of these things, then you know that he is probably enjoying the conversation, too. That's great. Keep it going!

★Try This!

Looking someone in the eye when you're talking is an important social skill. It shows the other person that you're interested in what she's saying. If you're looking around the room when you're talking with somebody—especially when it's her turn to speak—she may assume you're not interested.

Some kids have trouble making eye contact. If you have trouble with this, try looking at just one of the other person's eyes instead of both eyes at the same time. This can make it a little easier. Or look at her nose. Practice with a parent or sibling.

Here are some signs the other person might *not* be interested in what you're saying.

* yawning

* looking away from you when you're talking

* not saying anything about your topic or asking you questions about it

* checking a clock

* walking away or talking to someone else

If the person you're talking to is doing any of these things, it might be time to check with him to see if he's interested. You could ask directly by saying something like, "Do you want to talk about something else?" Or you could go ahead and change the subject by asking a question about what the other person likes or does. "What are your plans for the weekend?" Or, "What did you think of the substitute teacher yesterday?"

Here are good ways to switch the conversation:

* "What's new with you?"
* "So what have you been up to?"
* "What would you like to talk about?"
* "Sorry I'm doing all the talking—what's going on with you?"

If you ask questions and show interest in what other kids want to talk about, it will be more fun for them to talk to you. Chances are they'll want to talk to you again.

8 Keep the Conversation Going

Once the conversation gets started, keeping it going is the next step. That takes a little more practice. Remember to balance talking about yourself with asking questions about the other person. Don't talk too much about yourself, but don't overwhelm the other person with questions, either.

There's an old game called "hot potato." When you got the hot potato, you would hold it for a second and then pass it along—before it started to burn you! You didn't want to be the one who dropped the potato. Talking with someone is similar. When the conversation lands on you—like if someone asks you a question—your job is to catch it and throw it back quickly. In other words, you keep it going by answering or asking a follow-up question so you don't drop the conversation potato!

Here's an example of how it works:

* **Abby:** Hey, Zack. How's it going?
* **Zack:** Pretty good. Just getting ready for band practice.
* **Abby:** Yeah? What instrument do you play?
* **Zack:** The baritone.
* **Abby:** Cool! Is it hard?
* **Zack:** Kind of. But I like it. Do you play an instrument?
* **Abby:** I'm in choir.
* **Zack:** Oh, that's cool. How long have you been doing that?
* **Abby:** This is my first year. I might switch to band next year instead.
* **Zack:** I better get going. Mr. Hoffman hates it when we're late.
* **Abby:** See ya!

Did you notice how Abby asked a question, then asked follow-up questions after Zack answered? Then Zack asked a question ("Do you play an instrument?"), and it was Abby's turn to answer?

Sometimes you can pass back the hot potato just by nodding your head. Nodding your head when someone else is talking shows that you understand what the person is saying. It can also show that you agree with what someone says, or simply that you are listening. And it encourages the person to keep talking.

It's easier to pass the potato if you're listening carefully to what your friend is saying. If you daydream or look around while the other person is talking, you'll miss something.

The next time you say something, your response might not make sense in the conversation. The other person might feel bad that you weren't really listening.

A good way to make sure you don't get distracted—and to let the other person *know* you're listening—is to stay *active* in the conversation, even when you're not the one talking. Try making a short comment after the person

★**Try This!**
Practice having conversations at home with family members. Make sure they let you know how you do.

answers your question. This helps you stay engaged in the conversation. It also lets the other person know that you're listening, which makes him feel better about talking to you.

Sometimes just nodding your head and saying "Uh-huh" is enough. But you can take it a step further by saying something enthusiastic. Be sure to show enthusiasm in your tone of voice. Here are some examples:

* "Wow!"
* "Cool!"
* "Awesome!"
* "Sweet!"
* "No way!"
* "Sounds like fun."
* "Tell me more about it."

⑨ Join Group Conversations

Joining a group conversation can sometimes be harder than starting a conversation one-on-one. If you're sitting at a table at lunch and other kids are talking about a video game they like or a movie they saw, sometimes everyone is talking at once. It can be very confusing to know when to interrupt and when to simply listen. If you wait too long, someone else will jump in. If you start talking in the middle of what somebody else is saying, this will seem rude.

The best time to jump in is when there is a brief pause in the conversation and you have something to say that is related to what the other kids are talking about. Wait a few seconds before starting to talk. If you have a quiet voice, be sure to speak up so that others can hear you.

10 Say Good-Bye

Soon it will be time for the conversation to end. Maybe you've been talking for a while, and you can't think of anything else to say. Or maybe you have to leave. That's okay—conversations don't go on forever—but don't forget to say good-bye. Walking off without saying good-bye is not polite. Let the other person know you're leaving, and be sure to say something friendly to let her know that you enjoyed talking.

Here are a few examples:

* "See ya!"
* "Got to go—it was fun talking to you."
* "Take it easy."
* "Talk to you tomorrow."
* "Have a great day."
* "Catch you later."
* "Bye. See you tomorrow!"

Make sure to wait for a pause in the conversation. Don't cut the other person off while she's talking to say good-bye. And remember to smile!

? **What would you do?**

Remember Sasha from page 14? She was in a tough situation. She wanted to join some kids at their lunch table, but nobody invited her to sit down. What do you think she should have done?

In this chapter, you learned lots of smart tips for joining conversations. Use some of what you learned to make up a successful story for Sasha.

Quick Quiz

Let's see what you learned in this chapter.

TRUE or FALSE?

1 Nodding your head can let people know you're interested in what they're saying.

2 It's okay if you do all the talking.

3 You should only be friends with kids who share the same interests.

4 If someone looks away when you're talking to him, it might mean he's not interested.

5 Watching others can be a good way to learn how to make friends.

6 Looking a person in the eye when you talk to her will scare her away.

Now check your answers.

1. **True.** Just don't nod your head too much!
2. **False.** It's not fun for the other person if you do all the talking.
3. **False.** While sharing interests makes it more likely you'll become friends, you can learn about new things by having friends with different interests.
4. **True.** It might be time to start asking the other person questions or to end the conversation.
5. **True.** You can learn new skills by watching how others do it.
6. **False.** Looking a person in the eye lets her know you're paying attention.

You'll learn even more social skills in the next chapter.

Chapter 3

Seven Tips For Growing Friendships
(And Four Friendship Flubs to Avoid)

Haru started off fifth grade on a good note—he made two new friends. He talked with them on the way to the library and sometimes at recess. But after a few weeks, they didn't look for him at recess, and they didn't walk with him on the way to the library. They weren't mad at him; they just seemed less interested. He remembered to say "Hi" and asked them questions to get to know them better. But he wondered what else he might do to let them know he was interested in getting to know them better.

? What would you do?

Haru already has some basic friendship skills, but perhaps there are other skills he could learn that would improve his chances of becoming better friends with the kids he likes. After reading this chapter, see if you can figure out some extra social skills he might try.

In the early stages of a friendship, you're getting to know each other. That's exciting, but you're not really close friends yet. To grow your friendship, you'll want to be kind, honest, fun, and helpful—and be yourself! In other words, if you want to *have* a friend, you have to *be* a friend.

This chapter provides tips for building up a friendship—and a few mistakes to avoid.

tip #1 Share

When you offer to share a piece of gum or a snack, you show that you're thinking about the other person. That shows you care about him, which makes him feel good. If someone asks about your snack, it might mean he would like some. Sharing might be a good idea. Even if he says no, he'll still be happy that you asked. You can also share pencils, pens, stickers, or turns on your game system. Letting someone else try your game is a great way of getting to know someone. Just ask, "Would you like to try it?"

tip #2 Help

Helping people is another way of showing you care. Kids like to be around others who are helpful. Look for opportunities to help your friend—or anyone! Examples are if you see someone struggling to carry something, dropping something, having trouble opening a door, or looking confused or upset. Be sure to ask if the person wants help before helping, and ask what you can do. (Some kids don't want help or don't feel comfortable being helped.)

Here's how to do it:

> ✳ "Do you need help opening the door?"
>
> ✳ "Can I help you?"
>
> ✳ "You seem upset. Is everything okay?"
>
> ✳ "What happened? Do you need some help?"
>
> ✳ "This math work is pretty tough. Want some help? I think I understand it."

If you help someone and the person thanks you, be sure to say, "You're welcome!" or "Hey, no problem!"

tip #3 Take Turns

This is one of the more important parts of being friends. As much as possible, let others go first. It's always a polite thing to do, and it usually makes others feel good. Even if it's hard for you, you can't go wrong when you do!

If your friend lets you go first, remember to say, "Thanks!"

tip #4 Give Compliments

Who doesn't like to hear nice things about themselves? When you give someone a compliment, you show that you notice good things about her. That will help her feel good about herself, and she'll appreciate that you noticed!

The key to giving good compliments is making them specific. That means you have to pay close attention to people so you can notice things you admire about them. Examples are skills or traits they have and things they've accomplished. Make sure you pick something that you honestly like about the person. Most people can tell if you don't really mean it, and that can make people trust you less.

Here are a few examples:

* ✳ "Nice sneakers."
* ✳ "Great job in volleyball today."
* ✳ "That was a hilarious joke!"
* ✳ "Wow, you got a 95 on the spelling test? Way to go!"
* ✳ "Nice haircut."
* ✳ "It was cool how you stuck up for Liam today."
* ✳ "Wow—you're really fast!"

Try giving at least one compliment a day to people in your family, as well as your friends, teachers, or people you'd like to be friends with. Practicing it at home makes it easier to try with friends, and will help you get along better with family members.

One word of warning: It can be uncomfortable for people if you focus too much on how they look, especially if the person is the opposite sex from you. Save compliments about physical appearance for people you're already good friends with.

tip #5 Ask for Advice or Help

This is a great way to get to know someone better. Why? People like to feel needed and important. If you ask someone for advice or help, it means you trust him, and you think he's smart enough to be helpful. You're giving him a chance to be kind to you, which is always a solid way to build friendships.

Asking for help also gives you a great chance to return the kindness afterward. Thank the person and offer to return the favor. All this exchanging of kindness is bound to bring you closer—just because you asked for a little help.

What can you ask for help on? Here are a few ideas. Ask for help with:

* a school problem
* throwing a Frisbee
* making a gymnastics or dance move
* handling a problem with your parents or sibling
* a friendship problem
* a skateboard trick
* a book or movie recommendation

Here are some ways to ask:

* "Hi, Jean—way to go on the math test the other day! I'm not as good as you are at math. Would it be okay if I called you sometime if I'm having trouble with my homework?"

* "Hey, Martín! Can I ask you something? You're awesome on the basketball court—you make most of the baskets you try. Would you mind watching me shoot and give me some pointers?"

* "Can I ask your advice, Sam? My parents are getting divorced, and I know your parents went through that last year. Do you mind telling me how you dealt with it?" (If you're asking a personal question like this, do it privately so your friend doesn't feel embarrassed.)

Once your friend helps you out, here are some ways you can thank him or her:

* "Thanks for the advice, Cathy. That was really nice of you. I'll try it and tell you how it works out."

* "Thanks for the pointers, Manuel."

* "That's a great idea—I never would have thought of that. Thanks, Monique!"

tip #6 Develop a New Interest

People usually like being friends with others who have the same interests. If you don't have many interests, you may not seem fun to hang out with. So ask what people like to do for fun. If it's something you haven't tried, ask questions about it. It could be a sport like lacrosse or figure skating, collecting things like comic books, playing action games such as paintball or laser tag, or making up stories or plays. Choose something new that your friends do and give it a try. At worst, it gives you something to talk about. At best, you might love it!

Maybe you and your friend already have something in common, like reading or video games or movies. If so, that's a good way to help each other develop new interests. Make suggestions of books (or video games or movies) for each other to try. You can even lend each other the item. For example, you could say, "If you like science fiction, you might like this book, too." This way, you both develop new interests.

tip #7   Stick Up for Others

Part of being a good friend, and a good person, is standing up to kids who aren't being nice—especially kids who are teasing or bullying others. That's not easy to do, of course. If popular kids are making fun of your friend, you might worry what they'll say about you if you defend her. If tough or scary kids are bullying someone, it might feel dangerous to step in.

Sticking up for others shows that you have the courage to stand up for what is right. Even if the person being picked on or bullied is not your friend, sticking up for her shows that you don't believe in hurting others.

You can tell the other kids to stop, start a conversation with the kid being teased (showing her you care), or get the teasers to talk about something else (distracting them). Here are some ways to do it:

* "Knock it off, guys."
* "Hey, Vincent, don't worry about them. Come walk with me. What's new with you?"
* "Leave her alone—she's not bothering anyone."
* "Don't you have something better to do?"
* "Hey—who's going to lunch?"
* "Bullying can get you in trouble. You better quit it."

If you don't like when a kid is bullying others, there's a good chance that other kids feel the same way you do. If you stand up for someone who's being bullied, you might lose your

friendship with the one who is bullying. But you are just as likely to make more friends with others who agree with you.

Important! Sometimes you need to get an adult to help. If the situation seems dangerous or out of control, locate an adult right away. If it doesn't feel right, it isn't. At school you can find a teacher, counselor, playground aide, or principal to help. No one should have to put up with being bullied.

Check out StopBullying.gov for more information on how to handle bullying.

Four Friendship Flubs to Avoid

While there are lots of good ways to get along with others, some things will make getting along harder. Here are four things that can damage friendships.

Flub #1: Being Mean or Hurtful

It sounds obvious, but sometimes we are mean without realizing it. Or we end up acting hurtful when we don't really mean to. Do you ever do any of these?

* Grab people to get their attention

* Get too physical or rough when someone tells you to stop

* Steal or lie

* Say mean things about people behind their backs

* Make fun of others as a way of trying to be cool

* Pick on someone

* Bully others (name-calling, hitting, repeatedly putting someone down)

* Criticize others, telling them everything they're doing wrong

* Ditch one friend to hang out with another

Sometimes we might be feeling bad about ourselves, or we're having a bad day, and we take out our anger on others. Or maybe we're just trying to get a laugh when we do something mean. But it's never okay to make fun of others, bully them, or hurt them. You don't have to like everyone, but acting mean or hurtful says something about you that isn't good. When others see you being mean to someone else, they may wonder if you'll do the same to them.

> "If someone was being mean to my friend, I'd say, 'Please don't do that to my friend.' If that didn't work, I'd tell a teacher." —Boy, age 10

Flub #2: Being Rude, Gross, or Offensive

It might not seem obvious that it's unfriendly to make a gross joke or act rude. But it usually is! Just like treating someone cruelly, acting offensive can hurt a friendship. Here are some examples:

* Gross habits like farting, picking your nose, or burping loudly

* Swearing

* Giggling or laughing on and on without stopping

* Interrupting others while they are in the middle of talking to someone else

* Talking only about yourself and never asking others how they are doing

It can be tempting to act in some of these ways, especially when you're hanging out in a group. Maybe someone burps at the lunch table and everyone laughs. Or a popular kid talks about himself a lot. But don't be fooled. If you become known as the kid who belches or swears or talks about himself all the time, it makes you look bad to others.

Flub #3: Being a Poor Sport

Kids spend a lot of time playing games and sports, and it can get pretty competitive. People even compete over things like grades or who read the most pages in a book. A little competition can be fun if it's done with good intentions. It can drive you to play or work harder, and that's usually not a bad thing.

But when kids always act like winning is the most important thing, they're not fun to be around. Same with bossing others around, changing rules, cheating, and trash talking. Be careful to avoid any of these behaviors:

* Insisting that others let you join and play

* Telling people they have to play by your rules

* Cheating in games

* Bragging when you win

* Complaining when you lose

* Making excuses when you lose, like blaming the referees, the judges, or a teammate

* Teasing kids who mess up or don't do as well as others

Flub #4: Changing Who You Are to Fit In

Sometimes it's a great idea to go along with the crowd. If kids are doing something positive, such as helping people out, cheering for the team at a sporting event, or encouraging somebody who is feeling down, you can feel good about joining in. But it's never a good thing to change your beliefs or act in a way you don't like just to fit in. If kids are being mean, breaking rules, or doing something dangerous, listen to your

> "Just be yourself. Don't try to be someone you're not if you want it to work out." —Boy, age 8

gut. Will you feel proud to act this way? Will you be safe? What kind of person would that action or choice make you?

The same goes for changing how you dress or act. Copying a popular style might seem like an easy way to fit in. But trying to look like everybody else will not suddenly make everyone want to be your friend.

On page 38 you read about the importance of trying something new. And it's true—finding new interests can be fun and deepen friendships. It can even help you make new friends if you meet others who are interested in the same thing. At the same time, though, don't forget to be yourself. You don't have to make yourself into whatever others want you to be just to be their friend. Or pretend to like something just because someone else does. That's being phony, and it won't work in the long run.

Practice Makes Perfect

Learning all of these new friendship skills can feel pretty overwhelming at first. That's okay—it's normal. Practicing your social skills before you actually use them with other kids is one of the best ways to learn these skills. Be patient. You wouldn't expect to be a star basketball player on the first day of tryouts. You won't know all of your lines for the school play the first day of rehearsals, either. And you won't know all the answers on a test without studying first. It takes practice.

Who can you practice with? People in your family. Ask a parent to practice with you. Or even a brother or sister. Pretend that you are going to lunch at school and sitting down next to a new kid in class. Imagine that she does not know anyone at the table and your job is to get to know her. Take turns being yourself and being the new kid. This is called *role playing*, and it's a great way to learn new skills. After you do the role play, ask your family members how they think you did.

★**Try This!**

Have someone in your family record you practicing these skills on video. Then play it back and watch how you did. You might notice what you did well or what you want to change. It can be uncomfortable to see yourself at first, but it's a great way to improve.

?

What would you do?

Let's go back to Haru from page 33. He noticed that his two new friends didn't seem as interested in him after a while. What could he do to grow his friendship with the two boys?

In this chapter you read about several ways to make relationships stronger. Which of these would you recommend Haru try? What do you think would happen if he does? You decide.

Quick Quiz

Now you know a lot more about growing friendships. Check your knowledge by taking this short quiz.

TRUE or FALSE?

1 If it seems like everyone is doing something, it must be cool. So if kids are making fun of someone, joining in is a good way to make new friends.

2 Asking for help or advice shows that you are helpless and will make people avoid you in the future.

3 Belching the alphabet is a great way to make people like you.

4 Giving sincere compliments makes other kids more likely to want to hang out with you.

5 Practicing your friendship skills won't help—you should just do what comes naturally.

Let's see how you did.

1. **False.** That just makes you someone who bullies.

2. **False.** Asking for help actually shows you think highly of the person you're asking and may make him or her enjoy spending time with you.

3. **False.** Even if they laugh, most people will not admire you or want to be your friend because of this.

4. **True.** People like being around people who make them feel good.

5. **False.** Practicing with family members or even stuffed animals can help you do better with friends.

Chapter 4

Strengthen Your Social Skills—and Your Friendships

Gabi and Penny became friends when they were in the same gymnastics class, but the class is over now. While they always liked seeing each other, they haven't gotten together in a while, and they miss each other. Each is waiting for the other to make a move, but can't decide what to do next.

? What would you do?

What could Gabi and Penny do to keep their friendship going? You'll find some ideas for deepening friendships in this chapter. At the end of the chapter, you'll have the chance to make up an ending for Gabi and Penny's story.

Once you've found someone you like and get along with, you're on your way to having a great friend. As you spend more time together, you grow closer and more important to each other. This chapter is about making friendships stronger and improving your social skills.

Friendship Levels

Some kids like having lots of friends, while other kids like having only a few close friends. It depends on what feels right for you. One way to think about it is that you can have different levels of friends.

The beginning or first level we sometimes call *acquaintances*. These are kids you know by name and maybe have brief conversations with, but you usually don't hang out together. You're not going to invite them to your birthday party or a sleepover, because you don't know them well enough. But it can be fun to talk to them at lunch, play together on the playground, or even just say hi or share a joke in class (not while the teacher is talking, of course). Maybe in time, you'll become closer friends.

The second level you might call *casual friends*. These are people who you know a little bit better. You might play sports with them, hang out with them on the playground, or even invite them to your home for group events. Most of your contact with these friends is in groups, like at school, scouts, or sports.

The third level of friends is your *close friends.* Close friends are friends you like to be with a lot. You go to each other's homes, or out to a movie or the park. You call or text each other, and you feel very comfortable together. You share a lot with these friends.

The fourth level of friends is your *best friends.* These are kids who you trust to know personal and private things about you, friends you would help out no matter what. People often keep their best friends for a lifetime, even if they move away from each other. Best friends usually spend a lot of time together alone. That makes it easier to share important things with each other. You can have more than one best friend.

best friends

close friends

casual friends

acquaintances

Usually, new friends start out as acquaintances. As you get to know each other, you find that you have things in common. You enjoy each other's company, and you become casual friends or close friends. As close friends, you

> **"I have some friends I talk with in class. They're not close friends, but they keep me from feeling lonely."**
> **—Boy, age 13**

might start sharing a few more personal things and see what happens. This gives you a chance to figure out whether you can trust each other. If your friend shares personal things with you too, such as whether or not he still sleeps with a favorite teddy bear, this means that he trusts you. He thinks of you as a close friend, too. You don't want to let him down and tell his personal things to others, especially if it would embarrass him.

Start Slow, Then Get Closer

Usually, the progression from acquaintance to close friend—and even best friend—is pretty natural. You don't have to think about it much because it just happens. You and your friend like each other, so you spend more time together. On the other hand, if you find out you don't get along so well, you start to spend less time together.

It can be helpful to think about the four levels of friendship. For example, if you invite an acquaintance to a sleepover, that might feel awkward. If you leave a close friend out of your trip to the beach when you've invited casual friends, that will probably feel hurtful to your close friend.

As you become better friends with someone, you might be eager to become even closer. But take your time. It can take weeks or even months to really develop a friendship, so be patient. Once you've spent some time with your new friend, and you've decided you like the person a lot, invite him or her to do something outside of the place you normally see each other (like school). Fridays or the day before a vacation is the perfect chance to ask about this.

Not sure what to invite your friend to do? No problem! You can always keep it simple. "Want to hang out sometime?" is an easy way to find out if the other person wants to spend more time together. If the other person says yes, you can ask what she likes to do for fun. If you agree on an activity, then you can suggest some possible times.

You can read more about inviting kids to do things in Chapter 5.

Friends of the Opposite Sex, Different Backgrounds, or Different Ages

Most of your friends will probably be kids about your age who are the same sex as you. You will have more in common with these kids than anyone else. But having both guy and girl friends has its good points, too. You'll learn how to get along with both girls and boys, and that can help in situations like being partners on a class project. You can learn new ways of looking at things.

It can also be fun to have friends who are different from you in other ways. You may become friends with someone who has a different religion. Or you might make friends with someone of a different race or background. These differences can give you new ideas to think about. Even though you are different from each other, you will probably find that you have many things in common, too.

In the same way, having friends of different ages can also be enjoyable. You might learn something new from an older friend. Being friends

---

★ Sleepovers

Sleepovers can be a fun way of spending more time with your friends, especially close friends. Not all kids are comfortable sleeping over at someone else's home, so if you ask and someone says no, don't take it personally or think that he or she doesn't want to be your friend. Also, not all parents let their kids have sleepovers.

with younger kids can give you a chance to be a leader and teach them new things, such as how to play a game or solve a math problem.

With a younger kid, don't expect to play by the same rules as you would if it was someone your age. If you always win, it won't be any fun for the other person. Give your younger friend some extra points or extra turns to help make things more fair. This will keep things more fun for both of you.

Using Social Etiquette

Social what? Etiquette (ETT-i-kit) is the set of rules you use when you want to do the right thing socially. It's polite behavior that helps people get along better. You probably already know a lot of these rules, and using them when needed helps friendships keep going. Here are a few examples:

* Say "Excuse me" if you need to interrupt someone (or if you accidentally burp or pass gas).
* Say "Please" when you are asking for something.
* Say "Thank you" or "Thanks!" when someone gives you something—including a compliment.
* Say "You're welcome" when someone thanks you.
* Offer to take your guest's coat when he or she comes to your house.

There are other polite things you can do to keep friendships moving along. When you start getting to know people, say "Hi" when you see them. Not only is this polite, but it also lets your friends know you noticed them and think they're important. And it may help them feel more comfortable talking with you or hanging out.

Sometimes you end up being rude without realizing it. Maybe you've been talking a lot and notice that the other person looks bored. Or you accidentally let the door shut in your

> ★ **Try This!**
>
> Holding the door open so people behind you, or coming toward you, can go through is very polite. While it is especially important to do that for people who are elderly, who have trouble walking, or who are carrying heavy packages, you can do it for kids, too. You can even do it for adults such as teachers or parents. Look for chances to hold the door for people. This helps others and shows you are a caring person.

friend's face. Or you don't hear when your friend asks you a question, so you don't reply, and he gets mad. If something like this happens, that's okay—just apologize to let your friend know you didn't mean to be rude. Don't make excuses or try to make it sound like no big deal. Admit your mistake and move on. Keep it simple. For example: "I'm sorry—I was talking too much. What's new with you?" Or: "Oh, man, I didn't hear you—sorry! What did you ask?"

That's all it takes to show that your rudeness was an accident and you feel bad about it.

Showing Empathy

This is a key to making and keeping friends. When you have empathy, you are able to understand how someone else is feeling. But it's not enough to just understand someone else's feelings—you have to let them *know* that you understand their feelings. *Showing* empathy lets people know that you care about them and think about how they feel. It helps them appreciate you and feel close to you.

It's easy to show empathy when something good happens. If your friend just won a spelling bee, say, "Great job!" Put enthusiasm into your tone of voice. That helps show that you are excited for the other person. If your friend won a game, say, "Congratulations." That can be hard if you lost, but it's still important.

But it's even more important to show understanding, or empathy, when someone is not feeling so well. That's when your friend may really need someone to understand, which can help her feel better. If she fell off her skateboard and skinned her knee, she might feel a little better if you asked how she was doing or even said, "I bet that hurt!"

Here are a few other times your friend might appreciate your empathy. Show empathy when a friend:

* gets a bad grade on an important test

* gets injured on the soccer field

* loses an important championship game

* has to move away from his friends and family

* forgets her lunch

* has a family member or a pet die

* loses his homework

* isn't picked for a team sport she wanted to play
* is rejected by a friend or loses a friendship
* is picked on by other kids

You don't have to say a lot when something bad happens to your friend. But it helps to let him know that you feel bad for him. It shows you care about his feelings, which is one of the great things about having friends. Here are some things you can say when something bad happens to a friend:

* "Bummer—that really stinks."
* "That's got to be hard for you."
* "Oh no! So sorry to hear that. Do you want to talk about it?"
* "Aw, that's too bad. How's it going?"
* "I'm sorry that happened to you. Anything I can do to help?"
* "Ouch! That really hurts."

Staying in Touch

When people are good friends, they try to stay in touch. This is easy when you see each other at school every day, but it may be harder during vacations or over the summer. It's even harder if your friend is in a different class or school, or lives in a different city.

If you want to stay friends with people you don't see that often, it will take more of an effort to stay in touch. Otherwise you'll drift apart (your friendship will become less important). The good news is that it's easier than ever to stay in touch. You can call on the phone, send texts or email, send a note by regular mail, chat over the Internet, or even video chat. Do what's comfortable for your friend. If she texts a lot, that might be the best way to contact her. Other kids you might have to call on the phone.

If you have best friends you don't see often, you might contact them every day or a few times a week. With friends who aren't as close, once or twice a month may be enough. It depends on how you both feel.

Being a Good Sport

You've probably heard the old saying, "It's not whether you win or lose, but how you play the game." Well, that's kind of true. Of course you want to win—*trying* to win is part of the fun. But if you *have* to win to have a good time, then there's a problem. No one likes sore losers—people who complain or get upset when they lose. And it's not okay to make others feel bad by bragging or showing off when you win. That's a sure way to lose friends.

Here's a different way to think about playing, winning, and losing. If you like the people you're playing with, then their feelings are as important as yours. So it's important that they get to win sometimes, or playing won't be as fun for them. They probably like to win, just like you do. And just like you, they probably don't like feeling bad when they lose. Remember, the goal of playing a game with someone is to have fun.

Here are some good sportsmanship rules. See how many you already follow, and which ones you might try out.

1. **Pick a game that you both have at least some chance of winning.** It's not fair if one person always wins. If you are playing with a friend who is younger than you, pick a

> ★**Try This!**
>
> Keep track of your friends' birthdays by writing them in a calendar or planner or typing them into an electronic calendar. When someone's birthday comes around, help make the day special by saying "happy birthday," calling, or texting the person. That's a great way to show that someone is important to you. Gifts? Those are usually only for closer friends or if you're invited to a birthday party.

game that is better for younger people. For example, chess is better for older kids, but checkers is better for younger kids. If you are good at a game, help your friend out when he is first learning it. That makes it more fun for everyone. You and your friend can always teach each other new games, too.

2. **Cheer on your friend while you're playing the game.** You want your friends to feel good about themselves when they play with you. When someone makes a good shot, say, "Great shot!" Or say, "Great move!" or "You got me there!" if she captured one of your pieces in chess. If she misses a question in a game, or bowls a gutter ball, don't laugh at her. Encourage her: "Nice try. Maybe you'll get it next time."

3. **If you win, don't dance up and down and talk about how great you are.** That's rubbing it in and won't make the loser feel good. It's okay to be happy about winning, just don't overdo it. Shake hands with your partner and

say, "Good game." If you can think of something positive to say, such as "You had some great shots!" or "Maybe you'll win next time," this will help your friend feel better.

4. **Lose with dignity.** Tell your friend "Good game" or "You played really well," and don't make excuses for why you lost. For example, don't say the referee blew a call, you were really tired, you were distracted, the sun was in your eyes, or your stomach was upset from the pepperoni pizza you ate—even if those things are true. Let the person feel good about winning. Again, your friend's feelings are as important as your own, so if she feels good about winning, you can feel good, too.

Networking

One thing that grown-ups with good social skills do is help their friends make other friends. They call it "networking," and by doing this, people find jobs and make connections. Kids can do this, too. Everybody wins when you network. You help your friends by expanding the number of people they can get to know, and you might meet new people, too. Everyone gains more opportunities for fun, gets to learn about different things, and grows the circle of friends.

Here's how to do it. If you're talking to one of your friends and another person you know is nearby, introduce the two of them to each other. The easiest way to do this is to ask them if they know each

⭐**Try This!**
Write down the names and phone numbers or email addresses of people you want to be friends with. You can keep them in an address book or on your phone if you have one. This will make it easier to invite them to do things. It can be cool to print up cards with your name and number to give out to people you want to become better friends with. People who are good at exchanging this information often are better at making new friends and keeping friendships going.

other: "Hey, do you two know each other?" If you wait a second, chances are the two kids will introduce themselves. Or you can say, "Hey, Natalia, do you know Rachel?"

You can also introduce *yourself* to a friend of a friend. If your friend is talking with someone you don't know, wait for a pause in the conversation and introduce yourself. Just say, "Hi, I don't think we've met—I'm Cynthia." If you're shy, you can ask your friend to introduce you.

Another way to network is with activities or outings. Say you're going to a movie with two friends. If they know somebody you don't know, ask them to invite that person along. Parties, sports games, and other large-group activities are good places for networking. These are times when friends from different groups (like from your place of worship, school, or scouts) get together.

Avoid These Politeness Pitfalls

Here are a few impolite ways to act. Be sure not to do these things!

Laughing at Other People's Mistakes

Don't make fun of people when they make mistakes. That just hurts their feelings. Sometimes close friends can laugh when one of them messes up. That's a sign that you trust each other and you know that your friend doesn't mean to hurt you. It's great if you have a friend like this, but be careful. Sometimes your friend might get upset when you don't expect him to. If he does, laughing might make it worse. You can always laugh at your own mistakes, though!

Asking for Things

Don't ask for food or drinks at your friend's house when you first get there unless she offers it to you first. But if you've been there a while, it's okay to ask politely for something. Example: "Excuse me, may I have something to drink, please? I'm thirsty."

Don't ask if you can have one of your friend's toys or other possessions, either. It's okay to ask if you can pick it up or try it, and sometimes to borrow it, but don't take it without asking, and never ask to keep it.

Gossiping

Kids (and adults, too) sometimes gossip—talk about people behind their backs. They're usually saying bad or embarrassing things they wouldn't say to the person's face. Obviously, this is *not* polite and can be quite rude. Plus, it often backfires. After all, if you are talking trash about someone else with others, it gives the people you're talking to the idea that you might do the same to them. And if you say mean things about someone to a friend, that friend might say it to someone else. This can cause a lot of drama and cause you to lose friends. So try not to talk badly about others to anyone.

Spreading Rumors

Doing this is a lot like gossiping. Rumors are stories you hear people say about others that may or may not be true. Often these stories are mean, embarrassing, or hurtful. If you repeat these stories to other people, you are helping spread bad feelings. As with gossiping, this makes you look bad to your friends—they might believe you'll spread rumors about them, too.

If you hear a rumor about your friend, don't spread it. Instead, stick up for your friend and say, "I don't think that's true." You'll have to decide whether to tell your friend about the rumor. It could hurt his feelings to hear it. But he might need to know if people are repeating a seriously hurtful story about him.

Sharing Secrets

Maybe you have a friend who trusts you enough to share personal information with you. This is a real compliment! These might be secrets, things like who she has a crush on or that she still wets the bed. If a friend shares this kind of information with you, respect her privacy and be sure to keep it secret. Telling it to other people is one of the worst things you can do as a friend—and one of the fastest ways to ruin a friendship.

If you're not sure if it's okay to share something a friend told you, ask. As a rule, never share something that might be embarrassing to your friend. No matter how mad you are at your friend, or even if you stop being friends, never share secrets.

> Some secrets should *not* be kept. If a friend shares that she's being abused or is thinking about doing something dangerous, you need to let a trusted adult know. This isn't snitching or tattling—it is helping your friend stay safe.

Whining

We all complain sometimes—it's normal. Who hasn't complained about a parent, sibling, chores, or homework? But if you spend a lot of time complaining about stuff, your friends might start to think of you as a whiner. Whining can spoil a good mood and make people feel worse. It's okay if you're both sharing complaints about homework, parents, or other things. But if you're the one doing most of the complaining, and the other person isn't talking much, that's when it's time to knock it off and talk about something else.

PDAs

PDA stands for "public display of affection." Some people hug each other whenever they see each other. Close friends or best friends are more likely to do this than new friends or acquaintances. However, not everyone is comfortable with PDAs. It's awkward if you try to hug someone who doesn't like to be hugged. If you're not sure what to do, a handshake or high five is usually a safe bet.

? **What would you do?**

Remember Gabi and Penny? Did you notice that each of them was waiting for the other to take the next step? What could one of them do to help grow their friendship?

Using some of the social skills you learned in this chapter, make up your own ending to their story.

Quick Quiz

Take this quiz to see what you learned in this chapter.

TRUE or FALSE?

1 Being a good sport is important in making and keeping friends.

2 Acquaintances are the same thing as best friends.

3 Remembering someone's birthday is a way of showing you care.

4 If you are a girl, you should only have girls as friends.

5 Being a good sport can make others more willing to play with you and be your friend.

Now check your answers.

1. **True.** It shows that you are fun to play with and mature enough to handle losing.

2. **False.** Acquaintances are people you know by name, while best friends are people you share things with and hang out with.

3. **True.** Remembering birthdays usually helps others feel special.

4. **False.** It's okay to have friends of both sexes—you learn more about getting along with people that way. But it's up to you.

5. **True.** No one likes playing with someone who is a sore loser or brags about winning.

Chapter 5

Put Together Great Get-Togethers

Daniel, age 11, wants to invite a couple of his friends from school to a sleepover. His parents tell him he can have up to three people over. He's not sure who to invite because he doesn't want to hurt anyone's feelings. After thinking about it, he decides to ask three friends who have invited him to their homes, thinking that they might say yes. He gets up the courage to ask them, and two of the guys say yes, but one says no. He's disappointed, but realizes there will be other times.

While Daniel is very excited and can't wait for the day to arrive, it is the first time he's hosted a sleepover. He's nervous that things might not go well.

What would you do?

What advice would you give Daniel to make sure that his sleepover goes well? See if you can think of things as you read this chapter. You'll have a chance to make up an ending to his story later.

Doing things with friends is a great way to become closer. You can have sleepovers, go to a movie or museum, play at the park, go to the batting cages, go shopping, and a lot more. This chapter will help you get through all the ins and outs of inviting, being invited, and how to act in either case.

Inviting Others

One of the signs that a friendship is moving from acquaintance to friend is when you get together outside of school or other organized events. When you invite someone to your home or to go someplace together, you're letting the other person know

that you like him enough to get to know him better. After all, he'll know a lot more about you when he meets your family and sees where you live.

Before You Invite Anyone

Before inviting someone over, you'll need to figure out some things.

WHAT: The first step is to decide what you're going to do. Is it just going to be an afternoon to play board games? Is it going to be lunch? Maybe it will be a sleepover or a trip to the trampoline park. If it's your birthday party, you'll be planning for location, events, and food.

WHO: Who do you want to invite? Who do you have fun with or want to get to know better? If it helps you, make a list of people to invite. Ask your mom or dad what they think about the people you put on your list. They might have some ideas on who would be best to invite over.

HOW MANY: How many kids will you invite over? Inviting just one friend at a time can be easier. You can get to know that friend better, and you don't have to worry about making everyone happy at the same time. But some kids feel more comfortable having a small group of friends over. Ask a parent how many kids you are allowed to invite.

WHEN: Before you actually invite someone, ask your mom or dad when is a good day and time to have company. It would be embarrassing to make plans with friends first, only to have your parent say no.

The Invitation

Now, how are you going to invite people? For kids you see at school, asking at recess or lunch or during breaks might be good times. If you want to ask just one person, it's a good idea to do it when other people won't overhear. If you're having lunch in the cafeteria, or somewhere else with lots of people, other kids might hear you and get their feelings hurt about being left out.

If your friend lives in your neighborhood, you could simply ask her next time you see her. Or call her or knock on her door to ask (check with your parents first). Once a friend says yes, all you have to do is get her phone number or email address and give her yours.

> Be sure to get phone numbers of your friends before vacations, especially summer vacation, so you can stay in touch with them when school is out. Make sure you put the numbers where you won't lose them, or give them to your parents. If you have your own phone, put them in your contacts list.

Some kids may have a home phone that the whole family uses. Others may give you their dad's or mom's number. And some kids have their own phones. If you make a phone call, remember to be polite and use good phone manners, especially if a parent answers. This makes a good impression. Here are some examples:

* "Hello, this is Adam. May I please speak to Ben?"
* "Hi, Mr. Tanaka, it's Jamie calling. How are you? Is Saiki home?"
* "Hi, Maya, it's Sophie. Is this a good time for me to call?"

If your friend is not home or is busy, leave a message for him or her to call you back. Leave your phone number if your friend doesn't have it. Before hanging up, say, "Thanks. Have a nice day," or "Thank you, bye!"

Don't call too early or too late. Most parents won't like that. Many families have rules about how late kids can talk on the phone. Try not to call after 9 p.m.

If your friend has a cell phone, you can call or text. Keep it simple.

* **Calling:** "Hey, Cheyenne, this is Jessica. How are you? I was wondering if you wanted to hang out this weekend. I checked with my parents and they said okay for Saturday."

* **Texting:** "Hi, Cheyenne. This is Jessica. Do you want to come over this weekend? My parents said okay for Saturday."

If your friend says she can't, you could suggest a different day. If your friend says no again, you could say, "I understand. Give me a call when you have some free time." Be sure to end on a positive note anyway: "Maybe we can get together another time. Nice talking to you. Bye!" Or you could text, "Okay, we'll try another time."

Planning the Get-Together

Okay, let's say you've asked your friend over and she said yes. What will you do together? You could play sports, have fun doing hair and nails, watch funny videos, go to a movie, ride bikes, go bowling, play board games, do karaoke, or just talk. If it helps you, make a list before she comes over of things you and your friend can do. Pick things that you both might like. That makes it easier to get along during the visit.

If you and your friend disagree on what to do while you're together, it's polite to let your guest choose. If you and your friend start to argue and you can't work it out yourselves, or if you think your friend isn't playing fair, ask an adult in your family for help. This can help keep things from getting worse. Just say, "Hey Dad, can you help us work something out?"

> "When you invite a friend over, try not to cause problems. Always make sure you ask them if there is anything they need. Make sure that they don't get bored or feel left out, and that you treat them fairly."
> —Boy, age 12

If you have been doing what your friend wants for a while, and you're getting bored, it's okay to suggest a change. Remember to be polite: "Would you mind if we played something else now?" Be sure to thank your guest if he or she agrees.

Sometimes you have to bend a little to ensure that you and your friend have a good time. Maybe you don't want to play the game he wants to play. But he came to your house to spend time with you, so be flexible. You can say, "Sure, we can do that." Or, "How about we play the video game you brought now and then play Chinese checkers after lunch?"

Time to End

When it's time for your friend to go home, be sure to let him know that you had fun and that you'd like to get together again soon.

* "I'm glad you could come over, Marco! Let's do it again soon."

What if It Didn't Go Well?

Sometimes that happens. Maybe you had a fight or couldn't agree on what to do. Or maybe you just didn't "click"—you didn't get along as well as you had hoped. Sometimes you have to spend time with a person before you can tell if you get along well or not. You might have different interests. Maybe the person acted rude or didn't seem interested in doing things with you. Maybe your friend played with your sister or brother instead of you or didn't respect your things.

If things didn't go well, you can still be polite. Say something pleasant and simple, and don't promise to get together again soon if you don't want to.

* "Thanks for coming over, Keisha. See you at school!"
* "Hope you have fun the rest of the day!"

If things didn't go well because of something you did, be sure to apologize. If you weren't fair or you got mad, your friend may not be feeling very good about the get-together. But if you take responsibility and let him know you're sorry and that you'll make sure things go better next time, at least there's a chance that there will be a next time.

If you didn't like how the visit went but you want to stay friends, talking to your friend about it might fix the problem. Read Chapter 7 to find out how to talk to friends when problems get in the way of your friendship.

★Try This!

If your friends seem to like to play with your brothers or sisters instead of you, talk to your siblings and parents before they come over. Ask your siblings to do something else. Maybe your sister can have a friend over at the same time, or your brother can go to his friend's place.

When You Are Invited

Accepting invitations is pretty easy when you want to say yes. Here's how:

* "Sure! That sounds great!"
* "I'd love to! Thanks for asking."
* "Sounds good to me!"

Once you've accepted the invitation, the next step is figuring out the details. Find out what day and time your friend wants you to come. Get a phone number or email address so your family can check in with your friend's family to figure out details like transportation and timing. You'll also have to ask your parent for permission.

If you can't go but wish you could have, be sure to tell the person you want to get together another time. That lets him or her know that you're still interested in being friends. Here are some good ways to say it:

* "Oh, that sounds like a lot of fun! But I can't do it this weekend. Can we do it another time?"
* "Thanks for asking! I can't do it this weekend, but how about next weekend? I can check with my dad to see if it's okay."
* "Shoot! I really wish I could go."

Be sure to follow through and figure out a different day to get together so your friend knows you really do want to hang out.

Arriving at Your Friend's Home

When you arrive, be sure to greet your friend by name. "Hi, Jace!" will do just fine. Be sure to greet your friend's parents, also. This shows respect and is very polite. "Hi, Mr. King, nice to meet you!" If Mr. King says, "Call me Clarence," then next time you see him you can say, "Hi, Clarence. How are you?" If you've already met your friend's parents, you might say, "Nice to see you again!" Shaking hands is a bit more formal, but can also impress your friend's parents.

Being a Good Guest

If you want things to go well when you get together, and you want to be asked over again, follow these simple rules:

* Ask for permission before you touch things in your friend's house. If you see a toy you like, just ask: "Cool! Can I play with this?"

* Say "Thank you" for anything your friend or your friend's parents give you to eat or drink.

* Take turns deciding what to do. It's not fair if it always has to be your way. (It's true that the nice thing to do is let guests decide, but it's more fair—and more polite—to share.)

* You came to be with your friend, so play with your friend—not just his siblings.

* Be kind. Don't call your friend names or tease.

* Keep control of yourself. No running indoors or jumping on furniture. (But you already knew that!)

* If you start a game, finish it, even if you're losing. It's not fair to quit, but it is okay to ask to play a different game after you finish.

* Play by the rules. Don't change the rules of a game without agreeing on it first.

If your friend acts wild, acts like a sore loser, or cheats, it's okay to remind him of the rules or let him know you don't like it. But don't start an argument over it. If your friend keeps doing it, suggest doing something else instead.

★Try This!

Here's how to apologize:

1. Say you're sorry.
2. Say what you did and why it wasn't okay to do.
3. Tell the person it won't happen again.

Here's an example: "I'm sorry for cheating at the game. That wasn't very nice. I'll make sure to play by the rules next time."

You can practice with someone in your family so you'll feel comfortable apologizing. A written apology letter or card is also a nice idea, especially if you're apologizing for something big. It shows that you care enough, and are sorry enough, to take the time to write about it.

When Things Go Wrong

When friends get together, things don't always go smoothly. If you end up hurting your friend's feelings while you're at her house or apartment, if you accidentally break something, or if you break any of the family rules, apologize. That can save your friendship. Be sure to apologize to your friend's parents, too. If you don't apologize, they may not allow you to visit again.

When It's Time to Leave

Be sure to tell your friend that you had a good time. Also thank his or her parents for having you over. Here are some ways you can do this:

＊ "Thanks, Annika! I had a great time!"

＊ "Thank you for having me over, Mrs. Marelli. I had a lot of fun."

＊ "This was awesome! Thanks for inviting me. I'll have to have you over to my place next time!"

As you leave, and you're saying good-bye, it's also nice to say, "Have a nice day!" or something like that.

If you've been invited to do something special with your friend's family, it can be a good idea to send a thank-you note. You can buy thank-you cards at the store, or you can make them yourself. Maybe your computer has a program that will help you.

Keep Things Going

If you got together with your friend and had a great time, that's good news! If your friend invited you last time, you can be the inviter this time. That's a good way to keep the good times going—and the friendship growing. If you invited your friend over, chances are she will invite you over soon. If not, feel free to invite that same friend again.

As you get together with your friend more often, try doing things you haven't done already. If you always go to each other's homes to play, suggest going to a park, movie, or other fun place. You may discover new things you have in common.

?

What would you do?

Think again about Daniel at the beginning of the chapter (see page 63). How would you handle the big sleepover? As you learned in this chapter, there are things he can do to prepare, like plan a list of activities. And as long as he's polite and considerate, things will probably work out fine. Make up a story for Daniel that begins when his friends start to arrive and ends the next morning.

Quick Quiz

Take this quiz to see what you learned in this chapter.

TRUE or FALSE?

1 It's rude to just invite someone to your home. It's better wait for the other person to invite you first.

2 If a person invites you to his or her home, that means it's okay to ask for food as soon as you walk in.

3 Thank-you notes are a nice way to show your friend and his or her family that you had a good time.

4 Your friend should always let you pick the games to play when he or she comes to your home.

5 A good way to show your host how much fun you had is to throw yourself on the floor and beg and cry to stay longer.

How did you do? Check your answers.

1. **False.** Try taking the lead by being the first one to do the inviting.
2. **False.** It's better to wait until you're asked if you want something—that's more polite.
3. **True.** Thank-you notes are always appreciated.
4. **False.** As the host, it is more polite to let your friend choose the first game to play.
5. **False.** Actually, doing this is a good way NOT to get invited back!

Chapter 6

How Autism, ADHD, and Other Conditions Can Affect Friendships

Michael, age 9, is very excited about making new friends when he starts the new school year. He talks to everyone he sees in class and at lunch. Michael even talks when the teacher is talking and interrupts kids when they are in the middle of telling a story. At recess, he gets a little too rough and pushes the other kids for fun. He doesn't realize that they don't like being pushed. Soon the other kids start avoiding him. He wonders what he did wrong.

What would you do?

Michael seems to have a hard time controlling himself, and it's affecting his friendships. What advice would you give him? You'll find some ideas in this chapter, and at the end of the chapter you'll have the chance to make up a happier ending to his story.

Lots of kids have trouble making friends. But some kids have special problems or conditions (sometimes called "disorders") that make friendships even harder. This chapter explains some of these disorders, why they cause problems, and what you can do to help. Only a doctor or counselor can decide if someone has a disorder. If after reading this chapter you think you (or one of your friends) might have one of these disorders, talk to a parent or school counselor about it.

What's a Disorder?

"Disorder" is just a fancy term for problem. Some kids have disorders that affect their behavior and their feelings. It's not just kids who have disorders—adults have them, too. Some people with disorders take medication to help themselves. Others talk to a counselor to get help. Some people do both.

The following are some common disorders.

ADHD

People with ADHD, also called attention deficit hyperactivity disorder, have trouble paying attention. Often, they are also overly active and find it hard to settle down. They say and do things without thinking about what could happen. They may seem to talk too much, interrupt, not listen to what other kids are saying, and bother people. These things can be annoying to others. Kids with ADHD often are also disorganized, so it's harder for them to do things such as set up times to get together—they keep putting it off or forgetting to do it. Or they lose people's phone numbers so they can't call them.

Autism Spectrum Disorder

Kids with autism have a lot of trouble interacting with other kids. They have trouble looking people in the eye, carrying on a conversation, sharing interests, and understanding how others feel. They might say things like "I don't like your new haircut" without realizing it can hurt your feelings. People with autism often don't know how to read *body language*. This means that they have a hard time guessing how you feel just by looking at you. So, they might not be able to tell if you're interested in what they have to say. They might talk a lot about something even though nobody is listening.

Kids who have this disorder may talk strangely—for example, they may have an odd tone of voice or repeat everything you say. They may flap their hands when they get excited. Many kids with autism have a subject they are very interested in such as trains, dinosaurs, or maps, and they will talk about this subject nonstop—even if no one is paying attention or seems interested. Some kids with autism don't talk much at all or have little interest in having friends.

Kids with autism also tend to be overly sensitive to sounds, smells, or touch. If someone is talking too loudly, they might cover their ears, not realizing that other kids think this means they're not interested in what someone has to say.

Social Communication Disorder

Kids with this disorder have some of the same problems as kids with autism spectrum disorder when it comes to talking to other kids. They have trouble with body language, taking turns in conversations, and telling stories. They might not realize that kids usually talk differently to other kids than they do to adults. Understanding humor or jokes can be hard for them, and they often take jokes too seriously. Unlike kids with autism, they don't have trouble with being overly sensitive to sounds, smells, or touch, and they don't have the repetitive behaviors and narrow interests that kids with autism do.

Depressive Disorders

Kids with depressive disorders, like major depression, often feel down in the dumps. They might be grumpy or irritable, getting upset over little things. They don't feel like doing anything because nothing seems to makes them happy. They think negative thoughts, have trouble making decisions, don't feel very good about themselves, and expect the worst to happen. For example, they might want to talk to you or invite you over, but they're afraid to because they expect you to say no, which would feel even worse.

Bipolar Disorder or Disruptive Mood Dysregulation Disorder

Kids with bipolar disorder have mood swings. One minute, they may be joking around and be very happy. But the next minute, they may be angry and start yelling over nothing.

Or they might be in a good mood some days and in a bad or depressed mood on other days.

Kids with disruptive mood dysregulation disorder are very irritable and have severe temper tantrums over little things. Many kids with these disorders try very hard to keep their tempers under control at school, but have a harder time doing it when they're at home. This can be scary for someone whose friend gets overly upset about something small.

Learning Disorders (LD)

People with LD are often smart, but because their brains may work differently, they have trouble learning a specific subject such as reading, spelling, or math. This makes school harder for them. Their grades might be lower and they might not feel so good about themselves. They might have to spend extra time doing homework or meeting with a tutor, rather than playing or getting together with friends.

Social Anxiety Disorder (Social Phobia)

Kids with social anxiety disorder are very afraid in social situations. They worry that other kids will think badly of them or that they will do something really embarrassing, like saying the wrong thing. While they usually feel comfortable with people they know well, they have more of a problem with people they don't know well. They might get hot and sweaty, their hands might shake, or they might get a stomachache or headache. People with social phobia usually avoid social situations, which makes it harder to make new friends.

Remember, only a doctor or counselor can say for sure if someone has one of these disorders. If you have questions about any of them, ask your mom or dad, healthcare provider, or school counselor. One of these people may be able to help.

Being the Friend of Someone with a Disorder

Being friends with kids who have these disorders can be tough at times. Maybe other kids make fun of you because your friend is different. Or your friend with ADHD forgets to call you to get together, or interrupts you a lot when you're talking, which can hurt your feelings. It can be upsetting when your friend with bipolar disorder or depression gets really upset over little things. You might feel sad when your friend with social phobia can't go to a movie with you because he is afraid to be around so many people. It can be hard to talk with your friend who has autism if he only wants to talk about train maps. Maybe your friend with LD has to meet with a tutor after school, which means less time for playing with you.

But kids with conditions like these want to have friends, just like everyone else. And they can be good friends. You can share things that interest you and have a lot of fun together. Dealing with your friend's challenges can help you learn to be more sensitive, patient, and mature. Standing up for your friend teaches courage and shows caring. These are all great qualities.

If you are trying to be friends with someone with a disorder, ask that person about it so you can understand it better. Ask his permission first. "I was wondering about your ADHD. Would it be okay to ask about it?" Once you understand it better, you can try to be more patient—and helpful—when needed. The next time your friend with ADHD gets a little wild, you can remind yourself, "Oh, that's his ADHD making him hyper."

It's never okay to make people feel bad about their disorder or behavior. You can lose friends doing that—and it's just not nice. But do let them know if their behavior bothers you. Here's how:

* "Jon, you keep interrupting me and that bothers me. Can you please let me finish?"

* "Alia, I felt bad you didn't want to talk to my friends at lunch. Would it be easier if I introduced you to them first?"

* "Libby, it hurt my feelings when you yelled at me for dropping your bag. It was just an accident, but you really scared me."

If your friend tells you he has a disorder, that doesn't mean it's okay to tell everyone else about it. Maybe others already know. Maybe they don't. But many kids want to keep this information private. If they tell you, they are trusting you. If you're not sure if it's okay to share, ask your friend.

If You're the One with the Disorder

If you have one or more disorders, you'll have to decide if you feel comfortable sharing this information with a friend. If you're just getting to know someone, this can be a tricky decision. Once you share it, you never know who else might find out.

But having a disorder is nothing to feel embarrassed or ashamed about. It's sort of like being left-handed. Many people are, but most people are right-handed, so being left-handed makes some things harder. But it's something you're

★ **Medicine**

If you take medicine, make sure you take it the way your doctor tells you. Not taking medicine can make it harder for you to control your behavior. That can make a mess of your efforts to make and keep friends. If you don't like how the medicine makes you feel, talk to your doctor about it.

born with. Telling your friends can help them understand why you are having trouble. It might even help you stay friends.

Though having a disorder can make friendships harder, don't give up. It just means you'll have to work at it a little more than others. You may have to try harder to keep yourself under control.

It's important to know what challenges your disorder can cause. That way, when problems come up, you'll know why. But, while having a disorder can help explain your behavior, it's not an excuse to act out or hurt people. If you make a mistake, own up to it. Apologize if necessary.

Here are some not-so-good ways to deal with it—and some better ways:

* **Not-so-good way:** "Oops. That's my ADHD acting up. It's not my fault."

* **Better way:** "Sorry I got so wound up. I get that way at the end of the day."

* **Not-so-good way:** "You know I get angry a lot—why didn't you just let me go first?"

* **Better way:** "Sorry I yelled at you. I overreact sometimes. I try not to do that, but sometimes it's hard."

? **What would you do?**

Think back to Michael from the beginning of the chapter (page 75). His ADHD is affecting how he gets along with other kids. If you were a friend of Michael's, how could you help him? If you *were* Michael, what would you try to do differently? Invent a story in which Michael and a friend talk about his ADHD and help him improve his social skills.

Quick Quiz

So, let's see what you learned in this chapter.

TRUE or FALSE?

1 It's too much work to be friends with kids who have disorders. It's not worth it.

2 Understanding disorders can help you be more understanding of your friends.

3 It's never helpful to tell your friends if you have a disorder.

4 If you have a disorder like ADHD, it's okay to act however you want. After all, it's just your ADHD making you do it.

Check your answers.

1. **False.** Kids with disorders can be great friends. Plus, you can learn new skills by having friends with disorders.

2. **True.** Learning to be more understanding of others is a great friendship skill to have.

3. **False.** If you have a disorder, it's up to you if you tell. It could help your friends understand you better.

4. **False.** You are always responsible for how you act.

Chapter 7

How to Handle Fights, Hurt Feelings, and Other Friendship Troubles

Sarah has been friends with Muriel all year. They have played together and they often sit together at lunch. However, Sarah just found out that Muriel didn't invite her to her 12th birthday sleepover party. Sarah feels hurt and wonders if she did something wrong. Lately, she and Muriel haven't talked as much as they used to. Sarah wants to bring it up to her friend, but is afraid that she will upset her. She's also afraid that maybe the friendship isn't that close anymore. She's worried about what she'll find out if she asks Muriel what's going on.

? **What would you do?**

Would you bring it up with Muriel? Or would you ask your other friends what they think? Would you pretend that nothing has happened? Think about it as you read this chapter. You'll have a chance to make up an ending to this story on page 94.

All friendships run into problems sometimes—it's normal. Just like you probably don't get along with everyone in your family all the time, you're not going to get along with your friends all the time. Even though this kind of conflict is normal, it doesn't mean you can ignore trouble and expect everything to be okay. In fact, the way you handle hurt feelings, a fight, or an argument can make the difference between working it out and losing a friendship.

What Happened, Anyway?

Many times, conflicts with friends are caused by misunderstandings. Maybe you felt rejected when your friend didn't return your call or text. She didn't mean to leave you out, but it still hurt. Or maybe your friend seems to avoid you at school. Sometimes friends argue over the rules of a game or even which game to play. No one's trying to be mean, but feelings still get hurt. People sometimes do things without thinking about what could happen or how their actions affect others.

If you feel hurt by something your friend has done, don't assume she was hurting you on purpose. It could have been an accident, or maybe your friend didn't think about how you'd feel. Or maybe your friend was having a bad day—we all have those sometimes.

Of course, it's possible your friend is mad at you. But you can't know how your friend is feeling unless you ask. Often, this can be the hardest part of dealing with conflict. You wonder, Should I even bring it up? Do I call or text? Should I wait until I see her again and talk face-to-face? I'm so mad—should I just yell? Tell other friends what she did? Keep it to myself? Maybe I'll just avoid her.

When you are trying to decide whether or not to bring up a problem with a friend, ask yourself some questions. These can help you decide what to do.

* **How big of a deal was it?** If it was something little, maybe it's best to let it go, at least the first time.

* **Does it happen often?** If it happens a lot, it's probably hurting your friendship and is important to talk about.

* **Are you avoiding your friend because you're upset over it?** Avoiding a friend won't solve anything, and it could make things worse. If you're avoiding your friend, that's a good sign that it's time to talk about things.

* **How important is the friendship to you?** If the friend is very important to you, it's worth trying to work it out.

It's usually best to talk to your friend in person if you have a problem to fix. The bigger the problem, the more important it is to talk face-to-face. Don't do this in front of others—that can be embarrassing. It can put pressure on both of you to act differently than you normally would. For example, your friend might act like she's mad in order to look cool, even though she really wants to make up.

> "If I have a problem with a friend, I try to talk it out right after it happens. That way, you don't let it get in the way of your friendship."
> —Girl, age 12

Though you might want to, don't leave an angry message or send an angry text or email. You can't take it back once you send it. And don't post it online, such as on Facebook. Once you do, everyone can see what you said. That can hurt your friend even more—and make you look bad. Also, you can't see your friend's reaction. That makes it easier to say hurtful things. Try to think about whether you would make that comment to the person's face. If you wouldn't, it's not a good idea to say it by text or online, either.

Talking It Out

Whatever the reason for your disagreement, working it out is one of the most important parts of having friends. Conflicts happen, and learning how to handle them now will help you later in life. So working through conflicts not only can save your friendship, it can help you learn a big life skill.

When you're ready to deal with the conflict, find a good time to talk. Don't do it while your friend is rushing to class, in the middle of something else, or trying to catch the bus. Find a good time and ask your friend: "Do you have a few minutes? I want to talk with you about something important."

★Try This!
It can be scary to talk about problems. Even adults have trouble doing this sometimes. If you're worried about settling a conflict, write down what you want to say first, before you face your friend. Another option is to practice saying it to a family member.

What will you say? It's best to use I-messages. That's when you share your feelings by using the words "I feel" or "I felt." Add on a feeling word such as upset, mad, sad, hurt, and you have let the other person know how *you* felt. That works a lot better than accusing your friend of something or pointing out what he did. When you accuse, you say something like "You always ignore me in gym class!" If you do that, your friend will probably feel unfairly blamed and get angry back at you. That will only lead to a fight. Instead, use an I-message and say, "I feel bad when you ignore me in gym class."

Here are a couple of examples of how to start talking about a conflict with a friend. Notice how the speakers use I-messages to talk about their own feelings and don't accuse their friends of anything.

* "Hey, Mai, can I talk to you about something? I felt really bad when you didn't invite me to your party, and I don't understand why you didn't. Did I do something wrong?"

* "Grant, it really bothered me when you made fun of me in front of the other guys on the soccer field. I felt upset that you'd do that to me, and I don't get why you did it. Are you mad at me for something?"

In both of these examples, the speakers explain why they are upset and let the other person know that they are willing to take some responsibility. That makes it more likely the other person will want to talk things through. If you take some blame, chances are your friend will, too. (By the way, this also works with family members!)

When you talk with your friend, be sure to be respectful and calm in your tone. That will get a better reaction than yelling, name-calling, or putting down your friend.

> ✳ **Not-so-good way:** "You were a real jerk to me yesterday and it ticked me off."
>
> ✳ **Better way:** "Justin, I was really upset by how you treated me yesterday. Can we talk about it?"

Telling your friend how you feel is only the first step. It's just as important to listen to what your friend says. Your friend might get mad and blame you at first. He might bring up times that you upset him. Or your friend might feel really bad about upsetting you and apologize. Either way, listen closely and try to keep an open mind. You won't understand your friend's feelings if you interrupt or don't listen.

When Your Friend Is the One Who's Upset

If one of your friends is upset with you and wants to talk, the best thing you can do is listen. Even if what you did was an accident, or you didn't realize you were being hurtful, listen to what your friend says. Apologize for your role in the conflict, and let your friend know that you won't do it again. That's the only way to help your friend feel better, and helping him feel better is the only way to get back to being friends.

Even if you don't think you are to blame, an apology can help fix things. Apologizing is about making your friend feel better—not just admitting blame. On page 72, you learned how to give an apology. Remember the three parts: Say you're sorry, say what you did, and say it won't happen again.

> ✳ **Franco:** I really didn't like how you made fun of me the other day about my haircut being nerdy.
>
> ✳ **Tyler:** Sorry, Franco. I was just trying to be funny. I didn't mean to hurt your feelings. I won't do it again.

When you apologize, make sure you sound like you mean it. If you don't, your friend will know you are faking it.

Of course, sometimes it's not enough to just apologize. If you have hurt your friend, you will want to be more careful in the future. This is a great way to show you care and avoid hurting your friend again. For example, if your friend gets upset when you tease her about her clothes, promise not to do that anymore. And keep your promise.

★Stealing Friends

Some kids complain about other kids "stealing" their friends. It can hurt when someone new comes along and spends lots of time with one of your friends, leaving you behind. Who wouldn't be upset by that? But the truth is no one can "steal" your friends because friends don't *belong* to anyone. We don't own our friends. If your friend starts hanging out with someone else a lot and leaving you out, talk to your friend about it. Be calm and respectful. Here's one way to do it:

> "Olivia, it bums me out when you spend so much time with Sanura instead of me. It feels like you don't want to be my friend anymore, and I feel sad about that. Am I right?"

Forgiveness

To forgive means to stop being angry with someone and let go of feeling hurt or wronged. When you forgive someone, you are willing to apologize and also willing to accept the other person's apology. You decide to put what happened behind you. When you forgive, you turn a hard conflict into something that can help you be even better friends.

Forgiving can be hard, of course—even harder than apologizing. One thing to remember is that nobody is perfect. We all make mistakes, and sometimes we hurt our closest friends by accident. Forgiving one another is one of the best ways to not only keep friendships from ending over conflict but to actually make them stronger.

"Once, me and a friend got into an argument. We'd played a game at lunch with our drinks and I accidentally knocked her drink on the floor. She was really mad and we argued about it. We both felt bad. Later on, we both said we were sorry and we got back to being friends." —Girl, age 10

Fixing the Problem

After the apologies and forgiveness, there's one more thing left to do: fix the problem. If your problem was because of a misunderstanding, you and your friend can come up with a way to keep it from happening in the future. Maybe you promise to return calls sooner or not tease your friend about his lunchbox. Or maybe your friend promises to make room for you at lunch. Part of working out conflicts is to figure out things to do so feelings won't be hurt in the future.

How you deal with conflicts can make the difference between keeping and losing friends. When you're making up, stay respectful and watch your tone of voice. Even if you're still upset, try to stay calm. Yelling or arguing can wreck any chance of saving your friendship.

Unfriendly Ways

* ✳ "You're nuts!"
* ✳ "That's crazy—how can you think that?"
* ✳ "That's stupid."

Friendly Ways

* ✳ "Why do you think that?"
* ✳ "I see it differently."
* ✳ "I don't agree. Want to hear my view?"
* ✳ "I never thought of it that way—I'll have to think about that."

Sometimes it helps to take a break from the problem. If you can't figure it out today, just tell your friend, "Let's drop this for a while. Maybe we can figure it out tomorrow." Taking a break gives you more time to calm down and maybe see the problem from your friend's point of view. You are more likely to solve the problem if you think of how you can change your behavior to solve it instead of only focusing on what you think your *friend* should do. Friendship is a two-way street.

If you tried your best to solve the problems with your friend and nothing seems to work, then it's time to ask a grown-up for help. A parent, teacher, or other adult is more likely to help you if he or she knows that you've already tried to solve the problem on your own.

Here are some ways to ask:

* "Hey, Dad, can you give us a hand? We have a disagreement and we can't seem to work it out."

* "Ms. Lee, Nisha and I are having problems getting along at lunch and we keep getting into arguments. Do you think you could help us work it out?"

If you and your friend can deal with your conflict well and work it out, you may end up being better friends than before. After all, going through the hard work of resolving conflict shows your friend how important the friendship is to you. You might even learn something new about your friend by talking about it.

? What would you do?

Let's get back to Sarah and Muriel from the beginning of this chapter (page 85). Sarah is feeling like her friendship with Muriel is fading away, but she hasn't done anything about it. What do you think she could do? Make a plan to help her work it out.

Quick Quiz

Ready for this chapter's quiz?

TRUE or FALSE?

1 Many people get nervous talking to friends about problems in their friendship.

2 It's better to talk with friends face-to-face if you have a problem with them.

3 Apologizing when you hurt a friend's feelings is very important.

4 When you forgive someone, you turn back time so it's like the conflict never happened. Magic!

Here are the answers. How did you do?

1. **True.** Lots of people are nervous about bringing up problems, but practice makes it easier.

2. **True.** It's better than texting or talking on the phone because you can see how the other person is reacting. It's also harder to say something mean.

3. **True.** It's the best way to help your friend feel better.

4. **False, of course.** But forgiving *is* a great way to make your friend and yourself feel better.

Chapter 8

When Friendships End

Mark, who is in fourth grade, and Roberto, who is in fifth, have been best friends for a long time. They got together almost daily and enjoyed riding bikes, shooting baskets, and playing with toy soldiers in the mud by the creek. Then some new kids moved into the neighborhood who were a bit older and better at basketball. Roberto started hanging out with them more and stopped knocking on Mark's door to play. Now Mark goes down to the basketball court to join in, but the other kids usually tell him they already have enough players. Mark misses hanging out with Roberto. Lately he's been playing by himself at home. He wonders if he did anything wrong or if there is anything he could do to be friends with Roberto again. ▪ ▪ ▪ ▪ ▪

? What would you do?

Would you talk to Roberto about how you felt or just let the friendship fade away? After you read this chapter, you'll have a chance to revisit this story and make up an ending.

If you're lucky, some of the friendships you make as a kid will last for your whole life. But many friendships don't last that long. Often, you drift apart—you just don't have as much in common any more, so you hang out less and less. Other times someone moves away. Some friendships end because people fight more than they get along. These "breakups" can be hard, but they happen to everyone.

Why Friendships End

Friendships end for many reasons. People change as they get older, and they may meet new friends or develop new interests. Changing is a part of growing up, and sometimes it results in you not having as much in common with your old friend. You might notice that you don't have as much fun together as you used to.

Maybe you were close with someone when you were on the soccer team together, or in scouts or in the same class together. But when the soccer season or school year ends, you don't see each other as much. That makes it harder to keep a friendship going. You or your friend might not make the effort.

Moving away is one of the most common reasons that friendships end. One good thing about technology is that it makes it easy to keep in touch when you live too far away to do things together. Maybe you'll have some chances to visit your friend, but it might not be as often as you'd like. You can text, email, message each other, or even make video calls. Still, that takes plenty of effort, and kids may begin to lose interest once they start making new friends. If the friendship is important to you, you'll have to put more work into keeping in touch.

Sometimes friendships end because one person starts getting into trouble a lot and the other person doesn't. If your friend lies, cheats, steals, or starts hurting or bullying others, you might decide you don't want to be friends with someone like that. Your parents may complain that this friend is a bad influence on you. Spending time with people who make bad choices makes it more likely that you'll start doing bad things, too. Kids who are hurtful to others are more likely to get into trouble with the law when they become teenagers. You can try to help your friend stay away from that kind of behavior. If she doesn't want to change, it might be best to let the friendship end.

> "One friend of mine was a good student at first. Then she started being all bad, getting in trouble, and daring me to do bad stuff. I didn't like it. I told her, 'I don't think I can be friends with you anymore.'"
> —Girl, age 9

Some friendships are one-sided. This means one person does a lot more work to keep the friendship going than the other person. Maybe you keep calling your friend to get together, but she never calls you. Or maybe someone only wants to be your friend during the summer because you live by a really cool park. The rest of the time, she ignores you. That's not fair to you.

Your friendship might also end if you have a fight with your friend. If one of you does something to hurt the other—like if your friend spreads mean rumors about you—that can lead to a fight that's hard to get past. Mean teasing can lead to fights. Sometimes even competing in sports or a game can cause fighting. Most of the time, fights can be resolved. You and your friend apologize to each other and promise not to do it again. But sometimes the fighting is too serious, and you can't stay friends.

Signs That It Might Be Time to End a Friendship

Often, it's hard to know whether it is time to end a friendship. One way to figure it out is to see if it takes more effort to keep the friendship going than it's worth. If you're always fighting, for example, it takes the fun out of being friends. Or if problems with your friendship make you upset more than happy—especially if the same problems happen over and over and don't get any better—you might think about ending the friendship.

Here are some signs to look for when you are deciding whether or not to stay friends with someone. If your friend is doing one or more of these, it may be that the friendship is not a good one for you.

* **Lying**. If your friend tells you lies, especially if it happens more than once, this means you can't trust him.

* **Stealing**. Maybe you invite a friend to your house and find out later that he stole something of yours. As with lying, that means you can't trust this person and you might not want to remain friends.

* **Sharing your private information**. If your friend tells others about your personal information, such as who your crush is or something embarrassing, it's natural to feel hurt. Friends who don't respect your personal information are not likely to change.

* **Not making time to do things with you**. If every time you ask a friend to do something, the answer is always no, that probably means your friend is not very interested in you. It hurts, and sometimes ending a friendship like this is the best way to stop feeling hurt.

* **Breaking promises**. Friends who repeatedly break promises are friends you can't count on.

* **Hurting, teasing, or bullying you**. All friends fight sometimes. Maybe it even gets physical once in a while. You make up and move on. Friendly teasing and joking are okay, too—a sense of humor is a great trait in a friend. But if your friend often hurts you, makes fun of you, or hits or punches you, even after you tell him not to, that's not really a friend.

* **Telling you to do bad stuff**. If your friend tries to get you to steal, lie, hurt others, or try drugs or alcohol, this isn't a good friend or a safe person to hang out with. Talk to an adult you trust.

If your friend is doing any of these things, it's a good sign that it might be time to end the friendship. But if the person ever was truly a friend, you may want to give him or her a chance to work it out with you or apologize. Everyone makes mistakes. Maybe by talking the problem out, you can get back to being friends. Or maybe you'll find out that the friendship needs to end. Talking together may help you figure it out.

It's Time to Talk

It can be hard to talk about feelings with a friend, especially when you're upset with them. Lots of people don't like conflict. It seems easier to avoid the other person or just break off the friendship rather than talk about it. But if you're having a problem with your friend, the best thing to do is talk to her—especially if you're thinking about ending the friendship. It's not fair to just cut your friend out of your life, leaving her wondering why.

If you want to try to work it out, let the other person know how you're feeling about the friendship. Think of it as a "friendship checkup." Here are some ways you can start the conversation:

* "Hey, Deshi, what's up? Do you have a minute to talk? It seems to me like we don't hang out like we used to. I wish we still did, and was wondering if you do, too."

* "Leona, can I talk to you about something? I really feel left out when you don't talk to me at lunch—it seems like you only talk to your other friends. Is something wrong?"

* "Hey, Jacob, can we talk? How come you never call me back when I call you? It makes me feel like you don't want to be friends anymore. Is that true?"

If your friend says she's sorry for hurting your feelings or explains why she acted that way, you will probably start feeling better about things. That's great! By having the courage to talk with your friend about something important, you saved the friendship.

But sometimes this isn't enough. Maybe you don't think your friend really meant it when she apologized. Maybe she kept hurting you even after she said she wouldn't. Maybe the things your friend did upset you so much that you can't get past it and forgive. Or maybe your friend denies doing what you say she did, or she gets angry when you bring it up. It might mean the friendship is ending.

Some kids find it helpful to make a chart to help them decide whether to end a friendship. It might look something like this:

Reasons to Stay Friends with Janet	Reasons to End Friendship with Janet
We still have some fun together.	She never calls me.
We live on the same street.	She often cancels our plans to play together.
We have a lot of the same friends.	She makes fun of me.

After you've listed reasons on both sides of your chart, circle the reasons that are most important to you. This can make it easier to decide if you want to stay friends. If you're still not sure, try sharing your list with a parent or another friend you trust and see if they have any thoughts about it that might help you decide.

Could You Be the Hurtful One?

It's always possible that your friend is pulling away from you because you hurt his feelings or did something to upset him without realizing it. Maybe your friend is afraid to bring it up. If you notice your friend seems upset or seems to be avoiding you, ask him about it. Maybe it's something you can fix.

How? Just ask, "Did I do something wrong?" or "Did I do something that upset you?" Your friend might deny it at first, but if you don't believe him, ask again. "Are you sure?" A lot of people are afraid to tell someone when their feelings get hurt. Asking a second time might be enough to get your friend to admit it.

If your friend tells you that you hurt his feelings, it's important to admit what you did—even if you think it was no big deal. It won't help to say things like, "That was a long time ago!" or "That's not what happened" or "You need to get over it." Words like these run right over your friend's feelings.

Instead, let your friend know that you're sorry, that you still want to be friends, and that you'll try your best not to let it happen again. It's okay to explain why you did what you did or let your friend know you didn't mean it. But *start* with the apology.

* "Oh, shoot, I'm really sorry! I didn't mean to do that. Thanks for letting me know. I hope you can forgive me."

* "Wow, I feel bad. I'm sorry. I thought you were joking. I'm really glad you talked to me about it."

As you learned in the last chapter, being able to forgive is an important part of any relationship, including friendships. If your friend can't forgive you, it will be hard to stay friends. That's called "holding a grudge." Of course, if you apologize but keep doing the same thing anyway, your friend won't trust you anymore.

Ending a Friendship

Most friendships don't end with the kids deciding to "break up." More often, friendships just fade away. It might happen after a conflict or after you ask your friend about something hurtful she did. You have a talk and then things change. Or it might just happen on its own. You stop calling or spending time together, and you start to move on. If that happens, and your friend keeps staying away, you may just want to let it go.

But if you've decided to end the friendship, and your friend keeps asking why you don't want to hang out anymore, your friend has a right to know the reason. Telling her can be hard to do, but it helps both of you to put a definite ending to the friendship. Explain to your friend why you're ending it. Try to be honest but not hurtful. You might not be friends anymore, but this is still a person with feelings. Let her down easily.

Sometimes, friends try to convince you to stay friends. But if you have good reasons to end the friendship, be firm. You can stay kind and respectful while you remind the person of the reason you are ending it. Here's how:

* ✴ "I understand you want to stay friends, and I agree we've had some great times. But I don't want to be friends with someone who likes me only some of the time."

* ✴ "I can't put up with friends lying to me. That's not what friends do."

✳ "Sorry, Billy. I've decided I don't want to be friends anymore. I don't want to get mixed up in skipping school and stealing and all that stuff you're doing."

✳ "I just don't want to be friends anymore. I'm sorry, but my mind is made up."

After it's over, you will probably still see the person sometimes. Say hello and be polite when you do. And if others ask why you're not friends, try not to say bad things about the person. Just say, "Things didn't work out." It might seem really uncomfortable at first, but it will get easier with time. Don't start saying mean things about her behind her back or sharing private things about her.

If the two of you are in the same group of friends, things can get tricky. If you end a friendship with one person in the group, you can't expect everyone else in the group to do the same. That means you'll see your ex-friend while hanging out with the group. That might be hard for you. If so, consider spending more time with friends outside the group for a while. Let the gang know why they might not see you as much for a while.

★ **Is It Okay to Try to Be Friends Again in the Future?**

That's up to you. People and situations change, and things that might have caused problems in the friendship last year might not be so bad this year. If you miss your friend and see positive changes in him, you may want to give the friendship another chance. If your friend didn't apologize before, but later says he is sorry, this can be a sign that he has changed in a positive way. But make sure you're doing it for the right reasons. Don't try to be friends again with someone who hurt you because you have no other friends. If you're not sure whether to try being friends again, ask your other friends or an adult you trust. They might be able to help you make a good decision.

When Someone Else Ends the Friendship

If someone ends a friendship with you, it really stinks. Whether your friend talked to you about it or just stopped calling and getting together, you might feel mad, hurt, confused, or sad— or all of those. Yes, it stinks. It's hard and it's sad. It might not feel like it at the time, but you will make new friends.

> "One of my really good friends just stopped being friends one day. I think she just sort of moved on. At first I felt confused, but I figured she needed a little alone time and so I just made other friends. We still say 'hi' and stuff, but we're not close anymore." —Girl, age 12

You can start healing faster if you talk about what happened. You can talk with a parent or another adult. You can even talk to a friend or sibling you trust. Writing in a journal can also help. If you are up to it, think about what went wrong in the friendship and try to figure out what you would do differently. Reread this book for ideas.

Often, the best thing to do is to spend more time with other friends. You'll still feel hurt for a while, but connecting with other friends can help take the place of your ex-friend.

? **What would you do?**

Look again at Mark's story from page 96. It looks like Mark should talk to Roberto to find out what's going on. What do you think he could say? What do you think Roberto will say? Do you think he knew he was neglecting Mark? Make up two different endings for this story—one where the friends make up, and one where the friendship ends.

Quick Quiz

Take this true or false quiz to see how much you learned in this chapter.

TRUE or FALSE?

1 Friendships sometimes end because people change and grow apart.

2 It's better to avoid a friend you're upset with instead of talking about the problems.

3 If you stop being friends, you no longer have to be nice to each other.

4 If your friend is really mean to you, it's okay to tell everyone about her embarrassing blankie to get back at her.

Now check your answers.

1. **True.** Not everyone stays friends forever.
2. **False.** Talking it out first is a good friendship skill and can help save the friendship.
3. **False.** You can still be respectful, even if it's not easy at first.
4. **False.** Never share private information or talk negatively about your friend after the friendship ends. That would be mean, and it makes you look bad. Think of how it would feel if someone did that to you.

Chapter 9

The Next Step: Being the Best Friend You Can Be

CAROLINE, age 13, has been busy lately. She has basketball practice twice a week and a game every Saturday. She's a leader in her youth group, so she's helping plan the winter camp retreat. And she's been studying for the school spelling bee—she'd really like to win this year and go to the district final. On top of all that, Caroline has been spending lots of time with friends. • • • • • • • • • • • • • • • • • •

With all these things going on, Caroline didn't notice for a while that her friend Fina has been feeling lonely. Fina's best friend recently changed schools, so she doesn't see him anymore. And Fina hasn't connected with any other kids. She isn't involved in any sports or activities, so she spends a lot of time at school alone looking at her smartphone.

Now that Caroline realizes what's going on, she thinks, "I wish I could help her—but how?"

?

What would you do?

If you were Caroline, would you try to help Fina be happier? Or would you let her figure it out herself? If you wanted to help her, what would you do? You'll have a chance at the end of this chapter to revisit this story and make up an ending.

This book is all about making, being, and keeping friends. It has lots of ideas for helping you be a great friend. But you can do even more than that. You can be a leader—the kind of person people look up to. Anyone can be a leader—really! And it's not about being popular, smart, beautiful, rich, or good at sports. All you have to be is kind and generous—and sometimes brave—and look for ways to help others. This chapter shows you how.

Including Others

Not everyone is good at making friends. Some people are too shy, at least at first, to start talking to someone they don't know. You may know someone like this at school, in your neighborhood, in your scout troop or club, on your team, or in your religious group. Now that you've learned about making friends, you can take the first step in reaching out to those kids who struggle with making friends.

The next time you find someone playing alone or not being included in a group, you can invite that person to join whatever you're doing. If you're playing capture the flag on the playground and someone is alone, you can ask, "Hey, do you want to join us?" If she says yes, be sure to introduce yourself and the other kids who are with you. If your teacher wants your class to break into groups for a project, consider inviting that kid who always gets left out. Just about every class has a kid like that. It feels lousy to know you'll always be left out. If someone always sits alone on the bus or in the lunchroom, you could sit by her.

You might make people really happy, just by including them! And when you take the lead to help people belong, other kids might decide to do the same thing.

Organizing

It can be a lot of work getting everyone's phone number or email address, talking to everyone's parents, and doing everything else necessary to organize an activity for a group. But if nobody does it, you never do cool group activities. Maybe you and your friends think it would be fun to go skiing one day during winter break. It probably would! But if nobody organizes it, you'll never know. Why don't *you* organize it? If you do, you'll give everyone a chance to have fun. Your friends will probably appreciate it.

Being an organizer isn't that hard. Here's how:

1. Come up with an idea. Talk with your friends and see what everyone is interested in. Some ideas include going to a movie or an amusement park, skateboarding or

biking, having a sleepover, playing sports, or throwing a party. Maybe it could be a big round-robin video game tournament!

2. Get everyone's phone numbers or email addresses so you can contact everyone.

3. Check with your family to see what days and times work for them. Write them down so you won't forget. Having a calendar can help.

4. Make the calls to everyone and invite them. You might want to start with a smaller group first.

Remember, you can always ask a parent or other family member for help. Your parents may want to talk directly to the parents of your friends to arrange the event.

When you organize a fun event for friends, they may start to think of you differently. They might start to see you as a leader.

Mixing and Matching

Maybe you have some friends at school, some friends from karate, some from your dance class, some from your neighborhood, and some from scouts. There might be some overlap—like your best friend from school also plays second base on your baseball team—but a lot of these kids might not know each other. However, they do know you. If they like you, they might like each other, too.

Why not invite a few kids from different groups to do something? That way you can help your friends make even more friends—and you might make new or better friends, too. Even kids who know each other already might get to know each other in different ways. You might find you have more in common and more opportunities to do fun things.

Another way to help your friends is to simply introduce them to each other when you have the chance. Maybe you're talking with a friend at school and you see someone from your synagogue nearby. Call him over and introduce the two friends. Not only is this polite, but your friends might also become friends with each other.

Volunteering

Another super way to build friendships is to help others. People like being around others who are helpful. Volunteering also feels good.

You can help in little ways, such as taking notes and bringing home assignments for a classmate who is sick. You can also help in bigger ways. If you're good at math, you could offer to tutor someone who is having a hard time. Try asking your school counselor if there are students who could use some help. If one of your soccer teammates isn't so good at shooting, you could offer to practice with her.

You can even help in your community. By volunteering to pick up trash in your neighborhood or collect clothes and supplies for people who are homeless, you can make new friends as well as do a good deed. You can take the lead by asking a teacher, group leader, or parent to connect you with a volunteering organization or help you get something started. There are lots of opportunities for you to volunteer. You might assist in an animal shelter or community garden or kitchen, or start a homework help club or read to younger kids.

Look online at organizations such as VolunteerMatch.org and the RedCross.org for more information.

Standing Up

If you know someone is being bullied, you can help stop it. If you see it happening, say something.

* "Hey, Larry, leave him alone! He didn't do anything to you!"

* "Megan, quit teasing my friend. She doesn't deserve to be treated that way."

* "You better stop that. That's bullying, and you can get in serious trouble."

It's important to show the person who is being bullied that you care. You can do this in lots of ways. One good way is to invite them to hang out with you. Or, if the person gets bullied at the bus stop, go with him there and wait with him. Let him know that you care by saying something like, "You don't deserve that. I'm on your side."

If you know about bullying but don't see it when it happens, you can still do something about it. Be a friend to the person who gets bullied. You might even try talking to the person who is acting mean. Sometimes if you talk to someone when it's not the heat of the moment, the person will be more likely to listen to you.

If the bullying is dangerous—if it seems like someone might get hurt, or if you see a weapon—let an adult know right away. Trust your gut. If it seems dangerous, it probably is.

It can feel hard to stand up to bullying, especially at first. But the truth is that *most* kids don't like bullying, and they want it to stop. But just like you, they're afraid to say anything. You might find that if you stand up to bullying once or twice, other kids will appreciate it and look up to you. They will probably be glad you took a stand, and next time, they just might join you. That's how you can start to change things for the better.

? **What would you do?**

Go back and read Caroline's story from page 108. Do you think she is ready to step forward and be a leader? What can she do to help Fina feel better? Make up a happy ending to the story of Caroline and Fina.

Quick Quiz

Here's your last quiz of the book. Ready?

TRUE or FALSE?

1 You can be a great friend.

The answer? **True,** of course. Even if you've made mistakes before and hurt someone, or even if you're super-duper shy and scared of meeting people, you have lots to offer. You deserve to have friends, and you have the tools to make, be, and keep friends. The secret is to be thoughtful, be kind—and be yourself. Use what you learned in this book whenever you need a boost.

Remember to have fun, too!

INdex

A

Acquaintances, versus friends, 47, 48
Active listening, 28–29, 90
ADHD, *See* Attention deficit hyperactivity disorders (ADHD)
Adults
  apologizing to, 72
  friendships of, 10
  greeting, 70–71
  holding doors for, 52
  telling about dangerous situations, 40, 60, 114
Advice, asking for, 36–37
Age differences, 50–51, 55–56
Anxiety strategies for, 17, 30
Apologies
  after conflicts, 69, 90–91, 103
  for rudeness, 52
  strategies for, 72
Arguments, *See* Conflicts and misunderstandings
Attention deficit hyperactivity disorders (ADHD)
  overview, 76–77
  What would you do? story, 75–76, 83
Autism spectrum disorders, 77

B

Background differences, 50–51
Bad behavior
  ending friendships because of, 98–101
  rudeness, 42, 51–52, 59–61
  See also Bullying
Bad experiences, showing empathy for, 53–54
Best friends, 48
Bipolar disorders, 78–79
Birthdays, keeping track of, 55
Breakups, *See* Ending friendships
Breathing exercise, 17
Building friendships, *See* Growing and strengthening friendships
Bullying
  ending friendships because of, 100

mean or hurtful behaviors, 41, 98, 99–100
standing up for others, 39–40, 113–114
Burping/belching, 42, 51

C

Casual friends, 47, 48
Changing to fit in, 43
Close friends, 48
Comparisons with others, making, 8
Competitions and games
  ending friendships because of, 98–99
  losing, 55, 57
  sportsmanship and, 42–43, 55–57
Complaining, 61
Compliments, giving, 35–36
Conflicts and misunderstandings
  forgiveness, 92, 104
  handling and talking about, 87–91, 93–94, 101–102
  making a chart about, 102–103
  quiz, 95
  reasons for, 86
  What would you do? story, 85–86, 94
  See also Apologies; Ending friendships
Contacting friends
  phone calls and texts, 66–67, 88
  staying in touch, 54–55, 97–98
Conversations
  active listening, 28–29, 90
  asking questions, 21–23, 27–28
  changing topics, 24, 27
  ending, 30–31
  examples, 21, 22–23, 28
  interrupting, 24, 42, 51
  joining, 19, 29–30
  making comments, 22–23
  practicing, 29, 30
  quiz, 32
  signs of disinterest, 26–27
  signs of interest, 25

starting, 19, 20–21
talking about yourself, 24–25
things to talk about, 20, 23
What would you do? story, 14–15, 31
See also Feelings, expressing

D

Deep breathing exercise, 17
Depressive disorders, 78
Disorders, kids with
  definition of disorder, 76
  friendships with, 80–83
  quiz, 84
  taking medicine, 81
  types of disorders, 76–79
  What would you do? story, 75–76, 83
Disruptive mood dysregulation disorder, 78–79
Doors, holding, 52
Dressing to fit in, 43

E

Emails
  angry, 88
  contacting friends, 54, 97–98
Empathy, showing, 52–54
Ending friendships
  making a chart about, 102–103
  quiz, 107
  reasons for, 97–101
  talking about feelings, 87–91, 93–94, 101–102
  trying again, 105
  ways to handle breakups, 104–106
  What would you do? story, 96–97, 106
  See also Apologies; Conflicts and misunderstandings
Etiquette
  making phone calls, 66–67
  social rules, 51–52
Expressing feelings, *See* Feelings, expressing
Eye contact, making, 26

116

F

Farting, 42, 51
Feelings, expressing
  "friendship checkups,"
    101–102
  I-messages, 89
  showing empathy, 52–54
  talking about conflicts,
    87–91, 93–94
Fights, *See* Conflicts and
    misunderstandings
Fitting in, versus being your-
    self, 43
Flexibility
  choosing activities, 67–68
  turn taking, 35, 71
Flubs to avoid, 41–43
Foreign language words for
    friend, 9
Forgiveness, 92, 104
Friends
  age differences, 50–51,
    55–56
  background differences,
    50–51
  foreign language words for,
    9
  good things about, 1, 7–10
  kinds of, 11–12, 47–49
  opposite sex friends, 50
  stealing friends, 91
  See also Ending friend-
    ships; Growing and
    strengthening friend-
    ships; Leadership skills;
    Making friends
Friendship skills quiz, 2–3

G

Games, *See* Competitions and
    games
Gender differences, 50
Get-togethers
  ending/saying good-bye,
    68–69, 72
  inviting others to, 64–67,
    112
  planning and organizing,
    67–68, 110–111
  quiz, 74
  sleepovers, 50, 63–64
  What would you do? story,
    63–64, 73
Good-bye, saying, 30–31,
    68–69, 72
Gossiping, 59
Greeting people, 18–19, 51,
    70–71

Groups
  including others, 109–110,
    112
  joining conversations and
    activities, 14–15, 16–17,
    29–30
  organizing activities,
    110–111
Growing and strengthening
    friendships
  behaviors to avoid, 41–43,
    59–61
  networking, 57–58
  quizzes, 45, 62
  showing empathy, 52–54
  sportsmanship and, 42–43,
    55–57
  staying in touch, 54–55,
    97–98
  tips for, 34–40
  What would you do? sto-
    ries, 33–34, 44, 46–47,
    61
  See also Making friends
Grudges, holding, 103
Guests
  responding to invitations,
    70
  thank-you notes, 73
  tips and rules for, 70–73

H

Help
  asking for, 36–37
  for dangerous situations,
    40, 60, 114
  giving, in friendships,
    34–35
  volunteering, 112–113
Hi, saying, 18–19, 51, 70–71
Hot potato game, 27
Hurtful behaviors, 41, 98,
    99–100

I

I-messages, 89
Impolite behavior, *See*
    Rudeness
Including others, 109–110, 112
Interests, *See* Shared interests,
    identifying
Interrupting conversations,
    24, 42, 51
Introductions
  introducing others, 57–58,
    112
  introducing yourself, 19, 20,
    58

Invitations
  including others, 109–110,
    112
  inviting others to do things,
    49–50, 64–67, 73
  organizing activities,
    110–112
  quiz, 74
  responding to, 70

J/K

Joining an activity or group
  conversations, 14–15,
    29–30
  handling rejection, 18, 25
  how to ask about, 16–17
  including others, 109–110,
    112
  organizing activities,
    110–111, 112
Keeping friends, *See* Growing
    and strengthening
    friendships; Making
    friends

L

Laughing at others, 59
LD, *See* Learning disorders
    (LD)
Leadership skills
  including others, 109–110
  organizing activities,
    110–111
  volunteering, 112–113
  What would you do? story,
    108–109, 114
Learning disorders (LD), 79
Listening, in conversations,
    28–29, 90
Losing competitions, 57
Lying, 99

M

Making friends
  getting to know people,
    21–23
  greeting people, 18–19
  joining an activity, 16–18
  observing others, 15
  places to meet people,
    15–16
  quizzes, 2–3, 13, 32
  reasons for having trouble,
    11
  starting conversations,
    20–21
  through volunteer activi-
    ties, 112–113

What would you do? stories, 6–7, 12, 14–15, 31
See also Growing and strengthening friendships
Manners, *See* Etiquette
Mean behaviors, 41, 98, 99–100
Medicine, for behavior disorders, 81
Mistakes
laughing at others, 59
things to avoid, 41–43
Misunderstandings, *See* Conflicts and misunderstandings
Mood disorders, 78–79
Moving away, 97–98

N/O

Nervousness, strategies for, 17, 30
Networking, 57–58
One-sided friendships, 98
Opposite sex friends, 50
Organizing activities, 110–111, 112

P

PDAs, 61
Personal space, 21
Phobias, social, 79
Phone calls, making
contacting friends, 54, 97–98
good manners, 66–67
Polite behavior, 51–52
Poor sportsmanship, *See* Competitions and games
Positive self-talk, 17
Practicing
apologies, 72
conversations, 29, 30
social skills, 44
Privacy, respecting, 81
Problems, *See* Conflicts and misunderstandings
Promises, breaking, 100
Public displays of affection (PDAs), 61

Q

Questions
getting to know people, 21–23

in conversations, 21, 27–28
types of, 23
Quizzes
disorders, 84
ending friendships, 107
friendship skills, 2–3, 115
get-togethers and invitations, 74
growing friendships, 45
handling conflict, 95
making friends, 13, 32
strengthening friendships, 62

R

RedCross.org, 113
Rejection, handling, 18, 25
Role playing, 44
Rudeness, 42, 51–52, 59–61
Rumors, spreading, 60

S

Saying good-bye, 30–31, 68–69, 72
Saying hi, 18–19, 51, 70–71
Secrets, sharing, 60, 81, 99
Self-talk, 17
Shared interests, identifying, 16, 22, 38–39
Sharing, in friendships, 34
Siblings, 69
Sleepovers, 50, 63–64, 73
Social anxiety disorders, 79
Social communication disorders, 77–78
Social media, posting to, 88
Social skills
etiquette/social rules, 51–52
networking, 57–58
practicing, 44
rude behavior, 42, 51–52, 59–61
showing empathy, 52–54
sportsmanship, 42–43, 55–57
staying in touch with friends, 54–55, 97–98
Sportsmanship, 42–43, 55–57
Starting conversations, *See* Conversations
Staying in touch with friends, 54–55, 97–98
Stealing, 99
Stealing friends, 91
Sticking up for others, 39–40
StopBullying.gov, 40

Strengthening friendships, *See* Growing and strengthening friendships
Swearing, 42

T

Talking, *See* Conversations; Feelings, expressing
Teasing
ending friendships because of, 98–99, 100
sticking up for others, 39–40, 113–114
Texting
angry texts, 88
contacting friends, 54, 66–67, 97–98
Thank-you notes, 73
Topics for conversations, 20, 23
Trust, lack of, 99
Turn taking
in activities, 35, 71
in conversations, 22–23

V

Videos, practicing social skills, 44
Volunteer activities, 112–113
VolunteerMatch.org, 113

W

What would you do? stories
attention deficit hyperactivity disorder (ADHD), 75–76, 83
being a leader, 108–109, 114
ending friendships, 96–97, 106
get-togethers, 63–64, 73
growing friendships, 33–34, 44
handling conflict, 85–86, 94
importance of friends, 6–7, 12
making friends, 14–15, 31
strengthening friendships, 46–47, 61
Whining, 61

About the Author

James J. Crist, Ph.D., is a psychologist who specializes in helping kids and teens with ADHD, depression, and anxiety disorders. He also provides psychological testing and psychotherapy for individuals and families. He lives and works in the Washington, D.C., area, where he enjoys biking, swimming, sailing, and gardening in his free time. He also has a cool collection of frogs at home and in his office.